Tomasz Wójcik

POLAND
the most beautiful sites

*Z pozdrowieniami i nadzieję,
że wkrótce sam będziesz
mógł zobaczyć te miejsca*

*Ania i Paweł
z dziećmi*

Polska, styczeń 2008r.

POLAND the most beautiful sites

Author
Tomasz Wójcik
www.tomaszwojcik.pl

Tomasz Wójcik
fotograf

Translation
Ewa Kiszkurno-Koziej

Layout
Ola Lotterhoff

Cover design and composition
Olimpia Fudala

Copyright by BUCHMANN Sp. z o.o.
Warszawa 2008

ISBN 978–83–61048–09–1

Published by
Buchmann Sp. z o.o.
ul. Poleczki 9a
02–822 Warszawa
www.buchmann.pl

Printed and bound in
OZGraf Olsztyńskie Zakłady Graficzne S.A.
ul. Towarowa 2
10–410 Olsztyn

CONTENTS

ARKADIA IN NIEBORÓW

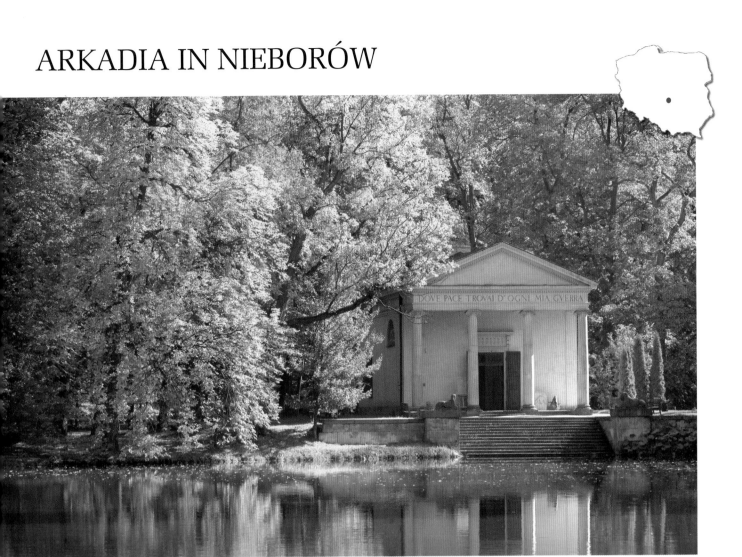

The palace in Nieborów was built at the beginning of the 16th century as a Gothic-Renaissance manor. At the end of the 17th century it had been bought by cardinal Michał Stefan Radziejowski, who erected on the same site a baroque building according to a design made by architect Tylman van Gameren. In the sixties of the next century Michał Kazimierz Ogiński, a new owner of the palace, reconstructed the interiors in Rococo style. During interwar period Nieborów, being the property of Janusz Radziwiłł, was visited by many famous politicians. Last owners of the palace were deported to the heart of Soviet Union after the II world war.

At the end of the 18th century within a short distance from the palace a romantic garden in English style, called Arkadia, had been established. It was founded by Helena Radziwiłłowa, and designed by Szymon Bogumił Zug. Name of the garden refers to antic myth on a imaginary idyllic paradise inhabited by primitive herdsmen leading simple unsophisticated yet happy lives. In the park one can find Sybille's cave, a gothic cottage called the Abode of Misfortune and Melancholy, a burgrave house, an aqueduct and temple of Diana with plafond *Jutrzenka* (*Aurora*) painted by Jan Piotr Norblin. Helena Radziwiłłowa collected in Arkadia a rich collection of antic art as well as Mediaeval and Renaissance artefacts. Majority of ob-

jects come from Petersburg collections as gifts from Catherine II of Russia, called the Great, the empress of Russia, partly from ruins of primate castle in Łowicz and purchases and exchanges with other collectors. In the 18th century Arkadia was considered one of the most beautiful gardens in Europe.

In 1945 Nieborów and Arkadia became a museum. At present one can admire the interiors, collection of sculptures, paintings, graphics, furniture and clocks in the residence. Also a book collection is impressive: a few thousand of old prints, among which the oldest Polish print, *Statut Łaskiego* published in 1506 containing strophes of *Bogurodzica* (*The Mother of God*), the oldest Polish religious hymn written in the 10th–13th century.

BARANÓW SANDOMIERSKI

First references to Baranów date back to the beginning of the 12th century. The town was situated near a ford in the Vistula River and its municipal rights had been granted by Casimir III, called the Great (*Kazimierz Wielki*) in 1354. The name of the town is probably related to sheep breeding, a possible profession of the then inhabitants. A convenient location near the Vistula river which was the most significant Polish commerce route, resulted in fast development of the town.

In Mediaeval times before the present castle a wooden stronghold stood being the property of Baranowski family Grzymała coat of arms. In 1578 the nearby lands passed into the hands of Leszczyński family Wieniawa coat of arms. It was one of the most outstanding Polish families: Stanisław Leszczyński had been chosen twice as the king of Poland in the first half of the 18th century.

The castle was built at the end of the 16th century according to a design by Santi Gucci and is one of the most beautiful Renaissance secular buildings of that time. The descendants of Leszczyński family rebuilt the residence, adding rich stuccoworks probably made by Giovanii Battista Falconi (Jan Baptysta Falconi). Significant changes had been made by Józef Karol Lubomirski, who ordered Tylman von Gameren to do renovation works in 1695. Between two towers of the west-

ern wing arcade-supported painting gallery was built, rich stuccoworks added, castle elevations modernized. In 1849 the castle including its furnishings was destroyed by fire, and its owners could not afford its restoration. In 1867 the residence had been bought by Feliks Dolański, who transformed one of the towers into a chapel decorated in Art Nouveau style with stained glass windows designed by Józef Mehoffer and a painting by Jacek Malczewski.

BIESZCZADY MOUNTAINS

B ieszczady is a very charming mountain range in Poland. This is a 1300 km long curved belt of the Carpathian Mountains. Bieszczady is also a region which is transformed by man only in a small part, but still attractive due to its mysteriousness, beauty of landscape and wildness of nature. On this area wolves, European bisons, deers, elks, lynxes or wildcats are abundant. Poorly accessible locations are refuges for brown bears. Their number is estimated at ca 25–30 animals, what constitutes ca. 70 % of all wild bears in Poland. It is believed that about 50 lynxes, 100 wolves and about 40 European bisons live wild in Bieszczady.

A typical feature of the Bieszczady landscape is high-mountain pastures above 1000 m asl. The most visited pastures are Połonina Wetlińska and Połonina Caryńska. As regards the flora of Bieszczady beech trees prevail contributing to 48 % of the forest area. A consequence of its unique natural values Bieszczady became Bieszczady National Park, which since 1992 is incorporated in the UNESCO International Biosphere Reserves.

Bieszczady was always a frontier area and the scene of clashing of Russian, Polish, Ukrainian and Hungarian impacts. After II world war the region became de- serted as a consequence of forced displacement of inhabitants to Soviet Union and to northern regions of Poland.

The most interesting monuments found in Bieszczady are numerous wooden Orthodox Churches, e.g. in Równia, Łopienka, Baligród, Żłobek, Turzańsk or Rzepedź. An important tourist feature is Solina artificial lake attracting lovers of sailing as well as other tourists because of its charming scenery.

BISKUPIN

Biskupin is an archaeological park known the best in Europe. The Museum is situated on a marshy peninsula in the Lake Biskupin, ca. 90 km northeast of Poznań. Excavations started in 1934 after discovering the piles tooled by human hand protruding out of lake water by Walenty Szwajcer, a local teacher. Archaeologists uncovered perfectly preserved fortified settlement of Lusatian Culture from before 2700 years. Excavation works which started in the thirties of the 20th century became the most important archaeological event in Poland; then Biskupin received name "Polish Pompeii".

Defensive settlement in Biskupin occupies an area of 2 ha. It was surrounded by bulwark 460 m long, of average width ca 3.5 m and height ca. 6 m. Along bulwark spreads a breakwater made of sharpened trunks, placed in a few rows. It is estimated that the inhabitants used 20 thousand piles to build it, i.e. four thousand trees. The village was accessible only from the south-west side by a pier 250 m long. The pier ended with wooden gate, towering above bulwarks, 3 m wide, playing the role of defensive and observational facility. Inside the village, close to the gate, there was a small yard – a place of meetings, gatherings and trading. Behind bulwark

there were built about 100 houses in 13 parallel rows. Average surface of the house was ca. 80 m². Each house consisted of vestibule and main room with bed for all the family members and a hearth. House interiors were opened to the south. Houses served as stores for crops, tools and domestic animals. Probably 7–10 people stayed in each house. The whole village could have 700 to 1000 inhabitants.

BRZEG

First mentions of Brzeg date back to 1234. In the place where town houses stand today a fishing and merchant settlement existed which was granted municipal rights in 1248. Urban layout of the town centre, designed at that time, survived until modern days. Rapid development of the town made it a capital of an independent duchy in 1311.

Precious historical houses reflect a long and interesting history of Brzeg. The most important are: the Castle of the Silesian Piast dynasty (Zamek Piastów Śląskich) built in Gothic and Renaissance style, sometimes called "the Silesian Wawel castle". The Gothic castle was first mentioned in the 13th century. Its present form is a result of the Renaissance style reconstruction by Italian architects Jakub Parr, Franciszek Parr and Bernard Niuron in 1532. The castle made its architects famous in Europe enabling them to start designing in other places, e.g. the Royal Castle (Zamek Królewski) in Warsaw, Kalmar castle or Uppsala Royal Castle in Sweden.

Finishing works in Brzeg castle continued until 1582. The entrance gate with beautiful sculptures representing founders' figures, busts of first Piast kings and Silesian dukes deserves particular attention. From architectural point of view the entrance gate of the Piast Castle can be compared to the most precious structure of the Polish Renaissance, i.e. Sigismund Chapel in Wawel (Cracow).

Another valuable building is the Town Hall built in the 16th century. Initiators of the project were the same Italian architects who designed the Castle of Piasts (Zamek Piastowski). The building is located on the town market square in shape of a horseshoe. Above the Town Hall a medieval tower dominates, modernized in Renaissance epoch.

Brzeg is also famous of its Gothic basilica, one of the greatest Gothic Silesian churches. St. Martin church was built on the turn of the 14th century. Formerly, the church had very rich wood furnishing and splendid stained glass windows. However, only fragments survived until modern times.

CIECHOCINEK

Ciechocinek is a very fashionable spa, biggest in Poland. The region where the town is located has low precipitation, high average temperature and large number of sunny days per year. Origins of the spa extend as far as the first half of the 19th century when exploitation of local saline sources began on a large scale. In the years 1824–1830 first salt graduation towers and salt works were built. Six years later salines had been applied to medical treatment on a commercial scale. In 1867 Ciechocinek was joined to a general railway network, and consequently the number of patients increased significantly. The town grew in a dynamic way – hotels, pensions, pump rooms, cafés and parks appeared.

Saline sources in Ciechocinek have unusual medical properties. They include a lot of compounds of calcium, sodium chloride, iron, bromine and many more microelements. Temperature of saline sources varies between 8 and 37 C and salinity between 0.19% and 6.43%. So far 19 saline sources have been opened which serve for healing baths, inhalations and alimentary purposes.

The most valuable monument of Ciechocinek related to the spa character of the town are salt graduation towers. Three unique wooden structures, enabling to evaporate water from saline, have been designed by Jakub Graff, a profes-

sor of the Mining Academy in Kielce. They had been built in the 19th century and were and still are the biggest objects of this type in Europe. They are as high as 15.8 m, and their total length is over 1700 m. The principle of operation of graduation towers consists in pumping the water directly from the source rich in microelements to the top of the wooden structure. From the top water drops down, filtering through graduation tower walls and under the influence of wind and sun it evaporates quickly, thus creating a microclimate rich in iod of medicinal properties in its surroundings.

CZĘSTOCHOWA

The name was given to the hill by Pauline monks who arrived from Hungary. They borrowed the term from parent St. Lawrence's monastery on Clarus Mons, Buda. Under the reign of Sigismund III and Władysław IV Jasna Góra had been surrounded by defensive ramparts. This very fortunate decision turned out to be very important during wars with Sweden (Swedish Deluge) in the 17th century, when 170 soldiers under command of abbot Augustyn Kordecki defended the monastery against the enemy. Successful defence of Jasna Góra was enormously important religiously and politically, becoming a symbol of struggle for national liberty. After II world war Jasna Góra turned into a symbol of fighting against communism. In 1979 John Paul II made a pilgrimage to Jasna Góra.

Pauline fathers arriving in the 14th century lavished attention upon miraculous painting of Black Madonna. According to the tradition the painting had been painted by St. Luke on a board taken out from the table the Holy Family used for partaking meals. Black Madonna has got two scars in the face the origin of which many legends tried to explain. Currently it is believed that the scars appeared in the 15th century when on Easter 1430 a gang of robbers had broken into monastery to steal precious votive offerings. They managed to loot St.Mary Chapel, took valuables and cut the Madonna face with sabres.

Placing miraculous painting back on Jasna Góra started the stage of pilgrimages. There were kings, nobles, knights among pilgrims as well as third estate. In particular, group pilgrimages on foot gained popularity. Every year the inhabitants of Żywiec made a pilgrimage since 1611, the inhabitants of Gliwice since 1627, and the inhabitants of Krakow since 1683. At present about 250,000 people take part in pilgrimages on foot to Jasna Góra every year.

CZOCHA

Czocha Castle was built on a rocky promontory in the valley of Kwisa river on the order of Czech's king Wenceslaus II of Bohemia (*Wacław II*). It was established in the years 1241–1247 as a stronghold guarding northern borders of the country. It changed the owners many times, remaining in longest possession of von Nostitz family for ca 250 years. Nostitz family rebuilt the castle several times finally giving it a Renaissance appearance. During the Thirty Years' War the castle was besieged by Swedish army but finally it was not conquered. In 1703 it became a property of Jan Hartwig von Uechtritz. At the end of the 18th century castle burned down because of unknown reasons together with rich furnishings and precious old prints library. However, it was restored quickly and after a few years it was ready to be inhabited again.

In 1909 Czocha castle was bought by Ernest Gutschow, a manufacturer of tobacco products from Dresden. Gutschow tried to raise his social status and to obtain knighthood; therefore, he immediately started rebuilding of the castle to be a future seat of the family. The works were supervised by a famous architect Bodo Ebhardt. Reconstruction was completed in 1914 giving the castle its present appearance. During the II world war the castle housed a school of Abwehra cryptographists and probably research laboratory of Werner von Braun, a creator of German rocket missiles, and later American space rockets Saturn, being a part of space project Apollo which aimed to land humans on the Moon.

After the war the castle was looted. In 1952 a military resort was organized there, what protected the building against further devastation.

A characteristic mysterious architecture became later a splendid set design to many movies. In the castle shooting of several Polish movies was taking place: *Gdzie jest generał* (*Where is the general*), *Wiedźmin* or *Twierdza szyfrów* (*Fortress of codes*).

FROMBORK

Frombork is a relatively small town inhabited by roughly 2500 people, picturesquely situated on Vistula Lagoon. The city was granted municipal rights in 1310. The most important object in Frombork is the Cathedral Hill, where are preserved basic elements of mediaeval architectural foundations. The oldest monument is a Gothic St. Mary's Assumption and St. Andrew Apostle Cathedral Basilica raised in the years 1329–1388.

Another important building which can be found on the Cathedral Hill is former palace of Warmia bishops. The building is Gothic and Baroque in style. Its construction had begun in the 14th century, the successive residents rebuilt the palace many times, re-creating its shape according to on-going artistic style.

The highest building of the Cathedral Hill is bell tower called Radziejowski Tower, raised in the second half of the 17th century. From viewing deck situated ca. 70 m above sea level a beautiful panorama of Frombork and Vistula Lagoon is spread. Lower levels of the Tower serve for exhibitions of modern art. In one of the rooms a Foucault pendulum has been hung up – the only instrument in Poland to observe rotational movement of the Earth. The lowest level of bell tower seats museum – planetarium.

A person strictly related to Frombork was *Nicolas Copernicus*. He was born in Toruń in 1473. When he completed his studies in Cracow, then in Bologna and Padua (Italy) he came back to Poland and settled in Frombork, a Warmian city, where he conducted astronomical observations and wrote his main book: *De revolutionibus orbitum coelestium*. Copernicus performed duties of a canon, bishopric administrator, inspector and medic. He developed a draft of monetary reform aiming to standardize Prussian and Polish coin. He died in 1543 and most probably was buried in Frombork Cathedral near one of the altars.

GDAŃSK

G dańsk was once the most populated and the most rich Poland's city. Its location at the Baltic Sea and membership to Hanseatic League in the years 1361–1669 made Gdańsk a city of many nations, cultures, religions and languages. At the times of Bolesław III Wrymouth, Gdańsk with Gdańsk Pomerania got under the rule of Poland. Some time later, after Świętopełk taking over the reign in Pomerania, it gained independence for a short period of time. In the 14th century the town passed into the hands of Brandenburg's margraves and Teutonic Knights and again was part of the Polish Kingdom in 1454.

Over centuries Gdańsk enjoyed many commercial charters becoming the largest Baltic harbour and one of the richest seaboard cities in Europe. In 1772 after the first partition of Poland the city was incorporated into the Prussian Kingdom.

Gdańsk history is related to many events affecting the history of the whole Europe. In 1939 the II world war started with artillery bombardment of Westerplatte stronghold, a Polish base, by *SMS Schleswig-Holstein*, a German battleship. Another event on European scale were strikes in Gdańsk Shipyard and signing the Gdańsk Agreement in August 1980 which led to the downfall of communism in Europe.

Despite vast destruction during the II world war the city is still full of historic monuments from various periods of time. Among the most interesting is Basilica of the Assumption of the Blessed Virgin Mary, the largest brick church in Europe, erected between the years 1343–1502, and the biggest mediaeval port crane called Żuraw, serving not only the cargo reloading purposes, but also as a device to put up ship masts.

Mariacka Street (St. Mary Street) deserves particular attention. It is one of the most beautiful streets and an example of rich municipal housing. The most important street in the Old Town is *Długa* Street (Long Street) setting up the Royal Way by connecting to *Długi Targ* (Long Market), presenting numerous historic monuments such as the Artus Court, Main Town Hall, Uphagen House or Neptune's fountain.

GDAŃSK THE ROYAL WAY

The Royal Way (*Droga Królewska*) in Gdańsk is a name of lined-up streets: Long Street (ul. Długa) and Long Market (Długi Rynek) commemorating ceremonious entering of monarchs to the town. The name is probably in use since ca 1457, when the king Casimir IV Jagiellon came to Gdańsk after defeating the Teutonic Order and incorporating Gdańsk into the Crown.

The Royal Way is also the main street and axis of the Old Town. Along this street the most important houses had been built, being now the most valuable historic monuments in Gdańsk. Houses in Długa Street have characteristic narrow richly decorated facades. Usually they belonged to rich merchants and important civil servants.

The most imposing secular building in the Royal Way is the Town Hall, i.e. the old seat of town authorities. It was built in the years 1379–1492. Inside there is richly decorated Great Council Hall (also called Red Hall). Interior's decoration is a work of Hans Vredeman de Vries and Izaak van den Block. The Town Hall has got 80 m high tower crowned by gold-plated sculpture of king Sigismund II Augustus.

Another significant building in the Royal Way is the Artus Court – a meeting place of the most rich merchants and citizens. It is one of the most splendid objects of this type in Europe. Its elevation is made in Renaissance style and decorated with images of Polish kings and statues of antique personalities. In front of the Artus Court there is a characteristic Neptune's fountain, symbolising a relationship of the town with the Sea. The originator of the fountain construction was Bartłomiej Schachman, a Gdańsk mayor. The fountain was set in motion in 1633 and today is a symbol of Gdańsk.

Another valuable monument along the Royal Way is the 18th century house of Jan Uphagen. According to the owner's will historic furnishings of the interior had not been changed for over 100 years, thus creating a characteristic for the epoch museum commemorating the life of rich Gdańsk burghers. The Royal Way is closed by gates: Brama Wyżynna, erected in the years 1587–1588 and Brama Zielona, which used to be the residence of Polish kings.

GOLUB-DOBRZYŃ

The castle in Golub-Dobrzyń was built by Teutonic knights in the years 1296–1306 on a hill close to river Drwęca. At the foot of the hill a town was set up which was growing buoyant until Polish-Teutonic wars in the 15th century. By the force of the Second Treaty of Toruń concluded in 1466 nearby lands and castle being so far a stronghold of southern border of Teutonic state passed to Polish hands.

The town prospered the best in the first half of the 17th century when the castle belonged to Anna, a sister of king Sigismund III Vasa. Anna Wazówna was born in 1568. Reportedly she was not a beauty; however, she was very high – over 180 cm. She was interested in botany and treatment by the use of herbs. She managed to grow a tobacco plant, for the first time in Poland. She spoke five languages, supported a scientific activity – e.g. she helped to publish *Zielnik* (Herbarium) by Szymon Syreński of 1600 pages. She died in 1625. For the reason of practising Protestantism she was not buried in Wawel but in St. Mary Church in Toruń which was in Lutherans hands at that time.

In the years 1616–1623 Anna Wazówna transformed the castle in Golub-Dobrzyń to a Renaissance residence.

Corners of the building were decorated with steeples, walls crowned with attic, and the palace itself was decorated with coats of arms. On the slopes of castle hill a garden in Italian style was established.

As a result of wars with Sweden in the 17th century the building was destroyed and never gained its splendour. It has been renovated in the years 1947–1953. Nowadays knight's tournaments and New Year balls take place here. It is a seat of a museum and hotel.

The most interesting are: a Gothic hall, horse stairs used to ride on horseback directly to palace rooms, a chapterhouse, an infirmeria and chapel (the only room on first floor which kept its original Gothic character).

STOŁOWE MOUNTAINS

The Stołowe (*Table*) Mountains are among the most beautiful mountain ranges in Poland. They belong to Sudety range and extend for 42 km. Its name comes from characteristic shape, which from a large distance resembles a kitchen countertop with vertical edges dropping down sometimes even 300 m. The Stołowe Mountains structure makes this example unique in Poland. These slab mountains are built out of cretaceous sandstones, which used to be a sea bottom. Due to orogenic movements sea bottom had been uplifted. As a result of erosion sandstone formed fantastic shapes resembling humans and animals. Wandering in the labyrinth of rocks one can come across e.g. mammoth, camel or elephant rocks.

The highest peak of the Stołowe Mountains is Szczeliniec Wielki (919 m a.s.l.) – dominating over the neighbouring rocky massif with numerous corridors and gorges in which one can find patches of snow until late summer.

In the 18th century due to its defensive significance Szczeliniec attracted attention of Prussians. At first they planned to build a fortress amidst the rocks protecting the neighbouring grounds. Fortunately these plans had been abandoned. In the same time the Stołowe Mountains became popular due to their tourist values. In the year 1790 the German emperor Frederick Wilhelm II came here. The mountains were also visited by Johann Wolfgang Goethe.

The first guide to Szczeliniec was Franciszek Pabel living in the years 1773–1861. During a visit of the emperor Frederick Wilhelm III he was appointed a royal guide and cashier of Szczeliniec Wielki – it was the first ever official appointment for a mountain guide in Europe. There were built, initiated by Franciszek Pabel, stony and wooden stairs leading to Szczeliniec and a Swiss-style tourist lodge called Szwajcarka on the top, existing until these days.

ŚWIĘTOKRZYSKIE MOUNTAINS

Góry Świętokrzyskie is the oldest mountain range in Poland and one of the oldest in Europe. Its name derives from the Holy Cross Abbey located on the peak Łysa Góra (595 m a.s.l.), where relics of the Holy Cross are kept. In 1950 the central part of the mountains became Świętokrzyski National Park. Its most characteristic feature is rock debris called boulder field (*gołoborze*). The area is covered by forests where fir and beech dominates.

The highest peak of Góry Świętokrzyskie is Łysica, informally called St.Catherine Mount (*Góra Świętej Katarzyny*) with its top at 612 m a.s.l. In the past Łysica was a central site for pagan worship. Today a cult wall of total length ca 1.5 km and height up to 2 m is still visible. There are reasons to believe that three gods were worshiped here. Therefore, to get rid of pagan cult faster, a Christian temple had been erected here and named after Holy Trinity.

According to legends Benedictine Abbey on Łysa Góra had been established by the king Boleslaw the Brave (*Bolesław Chrobry*) in 1006. The relics of the Holy Cross kept in the Abbey since the 12th century were a gift of St. Emeric, son of St. Stephen, king of Hungary. Since that time the Abbey became one of the most important sanctuaries in Poland. During partition of Poland the Benedictine Order was suppressed. Russian governors took over the buildings and converted them into a czarist prison of strict discipline. The prison existed until 1939. Since 1936 a part of abbey was taken over by Missionary Oblates of Mary Immaculate. At present, renovated post-Benedictine abbey includes cloistral buildings, Baroque-Classicistic church and early-Baroque Chapel of Oleśnicki family.

JAWOR

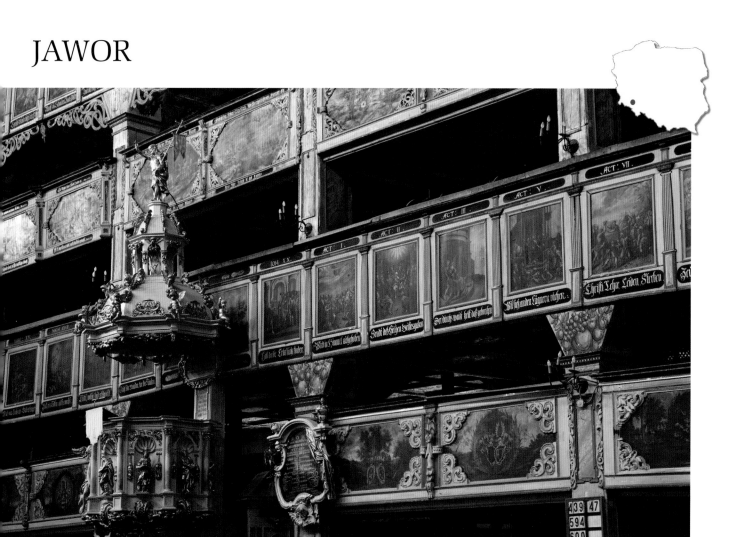

The name of the town derives from sycamore, a tree popular in the Sudety Mountains ("jawor" in Polish). The date of granting municipal rights is unknown, because the foundation charter did not survive to modern times. The most probable date is mid-13th century. At first the town developed well and quickly thanks to granted privileges, e.g. the storage right and salt trade right. At that time Jawor played an important administrative role as a place for assemblies of Świdnica and Jawor duchies.

Jawor declined during the Thirty Years' War. The town was completely burned. It was not until the 19th century when the town started to develop again. It prospered well until the II World War which ruined the town.

Jawor houses quite many historical buildings reflecting town's former significance. One of the most valuable is the Evangelical Church of Peace built in the years 1654–1655 by the agreements concluding the Thirty Years' War. Albrecht von Sabisch was a designer of the church which was built of very perishable materials (timber, clay and tar) but decorated in a splendid manner in Baroque style. The Church of Peace is the evidence of stormy history of Europe; there-

fore it has been entered on the UNESCO List of World Heritage in 2001.

Another historical building in Jawor is St. Martin church being the oldest temple in the town. It is a Gothic edifice erected at the turn of the 13th century.

The 14th century Town Hall is also worth seeing. Rebuilt many times, it took its contemporary shape in 19th century in Neo-Renaissance style.

Off the beaten track is the Piast Castle constructed in the 13th century. Destroyed during the Thirty Years' War has been reconstructed by Otton von Nostiz as a Baroque residence. Later it was modernized which unfortunately covered up its Baroque character.

33

JELENIA GÓRA

According to a legend the town's name originates from the times of duke Bolesław III Wrymouth *(Bolesław Krzywousty)*, who shot a deer king in local forest. He took the opportunity and established a town here with a deer in its blazon.

As a consequence of its location, Jelenia Góra changed rulers several times. For some time the town belonged to Czech Kingdom, later it was reigned by Habsburg family, and next was incorporated to Prussia. The town suffered economic up and downs many times. It was destroyed most heavily during the Thirty Years' War, the traces of which were visible on every building. The town prospered the best in the late 18th century, when the town became a significant centre of fabric production and tourist base for more and more popular tourist expeditions to Karkonosze Mountains.

Within the Old Town one can find many historic buildings from various phases of Jelenia Góra development. One of them is St. Erasmus and St. Pancras Church, the oldest in town, erected in the 14th century. The most important place in Jelenia Góra is its market place. There are many historic tenement houses with beautiful Baroque and Rococo elevations, as well as a Town Hall erected in the 15th century. The Town Hall was subject to many modernizations and rebuilding. In its present shape it appeared in the years 1744–1749 based on a design of Hendemann. At the beginning of the 20th century it was connected with neighbouring houses. In front of the Town Hall an early 18th century fountain was located with a Neptune statue, symbolizing relations of Jelenia Góra with overseas towns.

An interesting historic monument is Exaltation of the Holy Cross Church, a biggest church in town built in the years 1709–1718 which served as Evangelical temple. It can house ca 8000 people, and has beautiful interior. Unique, historic tombstones (unfortunately subject to destruction) of town personages surround the church.

KALWARIA ZEBRZYDOWSKA

S anctuary in Kalwaria Zebrzydowska is among the most famous pilgrimage sites in Poland. Cultural, scenic and architectural values of this place decided that in 1999 the sanctuary together with monastery and nearby chapels have become the UNESCO World Cultural Heritage Site.

Origins of the sanctuary dates back to 1602, when Mikołaj Zebrzydowski bequeathed the Calvary to Bernardine monks. In 1604 based on a design by Italian architect Giovanni Maria Bernardoni and Flemish architect and goldsmith Paul Baudarth the monks started constructing the church, monastery and chapels of the Way of Cross which later were enlarged by subsequent founders, i.e. Michał Zebrzydowski and Magdalena Czartoryska.

Kalwaria is Marian and Passion site known well in Europe. In August and September take place ceremonies in remembrance of birth and assumption of Mother of Jesus. During Holy Week are played Passion Plays commemorating last minutes of life, death and Resurrection of Jesus Christ, attracting streams of pilgrims. This liturgy had been taking place already at the beginning of the Calvary existence and its special order is preserved un-

til present days. The episodes are played by made up and disguised priests from the seminary. Ceremonies start on Palm Sunday by Jesus entering Jerusalem. On Maundy Thursday about 2 PM takes place the washing of the feet, parting with apostles and procession to Getsemani Garden. On Good Friday takes place a Caiaphas judgement, conviction of Jesus and the Way of Cross, in which participate thousands of pilgrims. Kalwaria mysteries are the oldest ceremonies of this type in Poland. It is considered that of all European Passion plays these are the most similar to mediaeval mysteries.

ELBLĄG-OSTRÓDA CANAL

Elbląg-Ostróda Canal is one of the most interesting technical marvels in Poland. It is the longest navigation route in Poland, linking Ostróda with the Vistula Lagoon. The canal is 127.5 km long, and change in elevation of the whole route is over 100 m.

The idea of building a canal appeared in the first half of the 19th century for transportation of crops and timber from East Prussia to the Baltic coast. Construction started in 1844. Its creator, designer and building manager was Georg Jacob Steenke. Opening ceremony took place in 1860, and the canal was ready reaching the town Ostróda in 1872.

The most interesting concept of the canal is five inclined planes helping to pull boats out of water in sections where the change in elevation is large. Boats were floated onto a special cradle car and then up or down on iron rails to the next section of the canal or next lake. Total length of railways is about 2 km. The longest one in Oleśnica is 479 m long, and a change in elevations is ca. 24 m. In addition to railways there are four locks on the canal. The canal construction took Moriss Canal in New Jersey (USA) as a model. Since Moriss Canal is not used any longer, water track Elbląg-Ostróda remains the only existing engineering construction of this type in the world at present.

During the most intensive operation of the canal the route was covered by several boats daily. In 1912 first voyages for tourists were organised. The canal was used as a commercial route still after II world war but development of roads made the traffic suspended. With exceptional scenic and natural values of the area a few tourist boats operates the canal nowadays – the route runs through the lake Drużno, one of the biggest hatchery sites of waterfowls in Poland.

The Canal was listed by UNESCO as a memorial to world culture inheritance.

KARKONOSZE MOUNTAINS

Karkonosze is the highest part of the Sudety mountain range. Its total area is ca 650 km², but only one third belongs to Poland, yet it forms the border between Poland and the Czech Republic. Large areas of the mountains are preserved as a national park by both countries. The most interesting features of the landscape, making Karkonosze alike high Alpine-type mountains, appeared during retreat of large glacial masses. Typical for such the landscape are postglacial kettles with vertical walls, tarns, peat bogs, boulder fields and numerous single rocks.

Karkonosze is the mountain range significantly transformed by man. Since ages people mined valuable metal ores and cut timber, leading to killing off big predators such as bear, wolf or lynx.

Karkonosze was first mentioned by Ptolemy, a Greek geographer, in the 2nd century AD. On his map the mountains are called Karkonotoi. Yet another name existed: Huge Mountains or Snow Mountains.

The highest peak of Karkonosze and the Sudety mountain range is Śnieżka (1603 m asl). Its slopes are covered with boulder field. A meteorological observatory is located on the top. The building is of peculiar shape resembling saucer; there is also a chapel, and a ski-lift station on Czech's side of the border.

The biggest towns situated at the foot of Karkonosze, playing mainly the role of accommodation centres for tourists, are Karpacz and Szklarska Poręba. The greatest tourist attraction in Karpacz is Wang temple. It had been built on the turn of the 12th century in Wang, a village in northern Norway. In mid-19th century the building was bought by Prussian king, Frederick Wilhelm IV. The king paid for it 427 German marks. After disassembling, transporting and reassembling in Karpacz the temple operated as Evangelical church since 1844. The Wang temple represents an excellent example of sacral Nordic wooden construction.

KAZIMIERZ DOLNY

Kazimierz Dolny is a small town, one of the most charming Polish towns. Its beautiful location and climate had been appreciated by painters coming here to seek inspiration in the 19th century. They praised Kazimierz, and brought thousands of tourists.

As early as in early mediaeval times on this area a settlement existed called Wietrzna Góra (Windy Hill). The village has been given to the convent of Norbertines from Krakow by the prince Casimir II, called the Just. It is probably them who, showing the gratitude for obtained domains, changed name of the village to Kazimierz. In the same time a castle was constructed on a neighbouring hill, of which only 20-m high tower remained. In the 14th century just below the tower king Casimir the Great ordered construction of a new bricked castle guarding the ford in the Vistula River.

The town developed in the 16th and 17th centuries getting rich thanks to crop trade. Renaissance houses were built then, preserved until the present day. Of particular attention are beautifully decorated houses of outstanding merchant families, e.g. of Przybył or Celej families and renaissance granaries situated along the river. Close to the regular market place there is a parish church of Romanesque descent. On the turn of the 16th and 17th centuries it has been modernized in Renaissance style. In 1620 the biggest organ in Poland at that time was mounted in the church.

Until the II world war numerous Jewish population lived here, who founded the 18th century synagogue, Jewish cemetery outside the town and kosher butcher shop. While staying in Kazimierz, it is worth visiting a nearby Three Crosses Hill (*Góra Trzech Krzyży*), from which opens a magnificent view of the town, the Vistula River and remains of the castle in Janowiec on the other bank of the river.

KŁODZKO

Kłodzko fortress is the most important fortification complex in Poland dating back to the 17th and 18th centuries. The stronghold standing on a hill Góra Forteczna was mentioned for the first time in 981 by Cosmas of Prague, a Bohemian priest, writer and historian in his *Chronicle of Bohemians*. In 1742 the fortress was conquered by Prussians, who enlarged and fortified the existing stronghold. In this shape it survived until present day. During II world war the fortress served as a seclusion for prisoners of war. Also a military factory was located here producing radio receivers and transmitters to V1 and V2 missiles.

It is rumoured that there are many unexplored so far corridors under fortress and town. Only 1 km of underground route (about 44 km in total) is accessible for guided tours. Presumably at the end of the war the fortress became a hiding place for pieces of art stolen by Nazis.

An interesting and characteristic object for Kłodzko is a rare historic stone Gothic bridge. Many historians think its construction had been started in 1281 and finished about 1390. The bridge is decorated with 6 religious sculptures endowed by Kłodzko residents. The sculptures are older than the bridge itself. The bridge is sometimes called *St. John bridge* or *Veit Stoss* (Wit Stwosz) *bridge* and is being compared to *Charles Bridge* in Prague.

Another interesting monument of Kłodzko is a late Gothic Virgin Mary Assumption Church. Its construction started in 1344. However, baroque style prevails inside. Of particular value is the main altar made in 1729 by Krzysztof Tausch, richly decorated pulpit made by Michał Klahr and the 16th century sculpture of *Kłodzka Madonna z Czyżykiem* (St. Mary of Kłodzko with siskin).

KÓRNIK

The first castle foundations in Kórnik were raised presumably at the end of the 14th century. Two centuries later thanks to Poznań province governor Stanisław Górka it became a splendid noble residence. It housed Henry Valezy travelling to Poland, among the others. In the 17th century the palace passed to the hands of Działyński family. In the 19th century Tytus Działyński decided on rebuilding the castle, giving it a neo-Gothic style. The body of the castle had got more romantic features in English Gothic style with additions of oriental architecture. Działyński collected numerous souvenirs of Polish glory with the intention to exhibit them in the castle after rebuilding. Construction of the residence and completion of the collection was continued by: Jan Kanty Działyński, son of Tytus, and subsequently, by Władysław Zamoyski. The latter just before his death in 1924 bequeathed his all possessions (including palace in Kórnik), to the Polish nation.

Castle in Kórnik is a monument on international scale, considered among the most beautiful examples of neo-gothic architecture in Poland. The 19th century interiors are of particular interest since they are preserved nearly in its original form. Among the most interesting are: a salon, Władysław Zamoyski room, the Armorial Hall and Mauritanian Hall.

Salon is renowned for richly gilded ceiling stuccoworks, a fire place, ornamented portals and marvellous floor. In the Armorial Hall there is a beautiful lacunar ceiling with 71 coats of arms of the 15th century knighthood. The most attractive in Kórnik castle is Mauritanian Hall decorated in three different styles. One can admire there a collection of Polish knights' and husars' armours, field marshal's batons, domestic objects of Działyński family and artefacts of sacral art.

A garden in English style of the area 33 ha adjoins the castle. Unquestionable attraction of the garden are pears growing on a willow.

KRAKÓW THE OLD TOWN

Kraków is the city visited the most willingly in Poland and very popular in Europe. Tourists are attracted here by its unique atmosphere and historic monuments accumulated since ages. Apart from ancient royal seat in Wawel Hill, the most significant tourist place in Krakow is its Old Town, a market square in particular.

Together with the whole network of streets branching off the market had been marked out in the middle of the 13th century after destruction of the town during Tartar's raid. The Main Square – the largest medieval town square of any European city – has an area of 40,000 m² (size 200 x 200 m). Still in Mediaeval times, in the centre of the market commercial warehouses called Sukiennice were constructed. With the passing of time they were subject to many transformations; the greatest in Renaissance times (the buildings were crowned with attic, mascarons and column loggias).

One of the most important sacral buildings in Poland – St. Mary Church – is situated on the market square. The church was erected in the 13th century and in the 14th century it had been rebuilt significantly. The most precious object inside the cathedral is a gothic altar made by Veit Stoss (*Wit Stwosz*) in the years 1477–1489. The church tower is the only tower in the world from which a trumpeter plays a bugle-call at full hour incessantly for over 600 years. Since 1927 St.Mary's Church bugle-call is transmitted by Radio Krakow becoming the oldest fixed radio broadcast in the world.

In Middle Ages the Old Town was surrounded by walls and many defence towers. In the 19th century majority of walls was disassembled, only historic towers and gates were left, e.g. representative Florian Gate, decorated with St. Florian's image and of St. Mary's painting. Also Barbakan was preserved, built in the years 1498–1499, being one of the biggest Gothic fortification buildings in Europe, a splendid achievement of military engineering art of the 15th century.

KRAKÓW WAWEL

Wawel is the name of limestone outcrop situated on the bank of the Vistula River in the very centre of Krakow. Since ages advantageous locations were places where humans settled. First historic rulers of Poland took Wawel Hill for their seat; therefore, it soon became an important political and religious centre of Christian Europe. Increasing role of Krakow during division of Poland into provinces in the 12th century made Wawel a seat of senior-duke, the most important among the dukes reigning the provinces of Poland.

Subsequent kings enlarged the castle. In the 16th century Alexander Jagiellon and his brother Sigismund I the Old changed the old stronghold into a magnificent Renaissance residence. Applied modern architectural solutions led to a breakthrough in the development of Polish architecture. The role of Wawel castle decreased when the king Sigismund III Vasa moved royal court to Warsaw in 1596.

A very important historic monument of the Wawel Hill is St. Stanislaus and St. Wenceslaus cathedral. At the beginning of the 14th century king Władysław the Short as the first Polish ruler was crowned in the cathedral to be a the king of Poland. After his death he was buried the-

re. It gave rise to a tradition of coronation and burial of Poland's monarchs in Wawel cathedral, thus creating a site of highest historical significance in the country. Here were buried bishops and later also famous persons with merits for the country, i.e. Tadeusz Kościuszko, Adam Mickiewicz or Józef Piłsudski. Side chapels were added to the main body of the cathedral, the most famous of which, considered a splendid achievement of European Renaissance, is Sigismund chapel (*Kaplica Zygmuntowska*) built in 1533 as a mausoleum of last Jagiellons.

Moving the capital to Warsaw and parting of Poland led to serious destruction of Wawel buildings. At the beginning of the 20th century renovation works started financed from private funds. At present Wawel is the most important historical and cultural monument of Poland and the most frequently visited site in the whole country.

KRASICZYN

The castle in Krasiczyn is one of the most beautiful monuments of renaissance and mannerism architecture in Poland and one of the most magnificent Europe's castles. Construction of the residence was started by Stanisław Krasicki in 1580, and was finished by his son Marcin in 1631.

The building plan is square-shaped. From the northern and eastern side there are residential wings and from the south and west screening walls decorated with openwork attic. There are four round towers in the castle corners called respectively: "Boska" (of God), "Papieska" (of Pope), "Królewska" (of King) and "Szlachecka" (of Noble). The names correspond to world importance hierarchy declared by Krasicki family. The graphite decorations representing images of Polish kings, biblical and hunting scenes are unique on the world scale. They occupy an area of ca. 7000 m². Another precious architectural object is a chapel located in tower "Boska", sometimes compared to Sigismund chapel in Wawel.

Krasiczyn was visited by Polish kings many times, e.g. Sigismund III Vasa (*Zygmunt III Waza*), John II Casimir (*Jan Kazimierz*) and Augustus II the Strong (*August II*). In 1835 the palace was bought by prince Leon Sapieha. At that time also Jan Matejko stayed in the castle, preparing sketches to his painting *Bitwa pod Grunwaldem* (*Battle of Grunwalds*). In order to paint the main character, i.e. prince Vytautas the Great, also known by the traditional Polish and German name Prince Witold, Adam Sapieha (called "red prince") posed for.

A beautiful park surrounds the palace, full of exotic trees and shrubs. Typical for the park are old oak and linden trees which were planted when a new baby was born in the family: oak trees for a boy, linden trees for a girl.

In 1867 in Krasiczyn Adam cardinal Sapieha was born, from the hands of whom Karol Wojtyła received holy orders. The castle remained in the hands of Sapieha family until 1944. Nowadays it seats a museum, a hotel and restaurant.

KRZESZÓW

Krzeszów is a small village in Middle Sudety Mountains on Zadrna River. In 1242 duchess Anna, a widow of Henry the Pious, brought here Benedictine monks from Bohemian Opatovice, funding a monastery for them. Soon the monks sold the castle to Bolko I, duke of Świdnica who established here a Cistercians abbey in 1292.

Prosperity of Krzeszów fell in mid-17th century during lifetime of abbot Bernardus Ros, who renovated buildings destroyed during Hussite invasions in the 15th century. New buildings were constructed, i.e. St. Joseph church or stations of the Way of Cross. A period of marvellous development was coming to a close when Silesia region was taken over by Prussia. In 1810 on the order of Prussian king the abbey was dissolved, monks exiled, and properties confiscated. Only in 1924 after taking over by Bernardine monks the monastery began to restore its former splendour. After the II world war Benedictine nuns from Lvov settled here, and Cistercian monks administer local cure since 1970.

Monastic complex in Krzeszów is one of the most beautiful Baroque relics in Silesia, considered priceless. Therefore, it is expected to enter the complex to the UNESCO World Heritage List in the future. The most important objects are Minor Basilica of St. Mary Assumption which houses the most precious treasure of Legnica diocese, i.e. icon of Graceful St. Mary, also called the Queen of Sudety. This painting is one of the oldest in Europe and the oldest in Poland 13th century painting of Madonna. Of particular attention is also richly decorated basilica façade with huge statues of angels and patron saints. The church plays the role of mausoleum of Piast dukes of Świdnica and Jawor region. Here are buried: Bolko II the Small, Bernard of Świdnica, Henry I of Jawor, Henry II of Świdnica, Bolko II and probably Bolko III.

Another valuable relic is also St. Joseph church from late 17th century and the Way of Cross consisting of 33 bricked stations situated on the area of the monastery and around Krzeszów. Outside the village one can see rarely found penitential crosses, placed as a part of penance in crime sites.

KSIĄŻ

The castle in Książ is the third greatest after Malbork and Wawel castle in Poland. There are about 400 rooms of total cubage ca. 150 thous. m^3. First building here was erected in the years 1288–1292 by Bolesław I the Stern (*Bolesław I Surowy*), prince of Świdnica and Jaworze province. It was funded together with many other strongholds in order to protect principality borders. In 1509 the castle was handed over to family Hochberg as a fee by Polish king Vladislaus II of Bohemia and Hungary (*Władysław Jagiellończyk*), also known as Ladislaus Jagiellon. One hundred years later the family of Hochberg bought out their properties and since that time Książ became a hereditary property of the family.

In the years 1705–1732 the then owner Konrad Ernest Maksymilian von Hochberg began rebuilding of the castle giving it a baroque character. Eastern fronton and representative hall called Maximilian Hall was built at that time. In the 19th century the family of Hochbergs were granted a princehood, and later, due to family and marital relations and financial investments, became one of the most rich families in Europe. Książ was visited by Francis Joseph I, the emperor of Austria (*Franciszek Józef*), Frederick Wilhelm III, king of Prussia, Nicholas I, the emperor of Russia and Sir Winston Leonard Spencer-Churchill, a British politician who served as Prime Minister of the United Kingdom.

At the beginning of the 20th century the castle was extended with a huge wing from north-west side. During the II world war it was occupied by German troops. Several thousand of workers from Todt's paramilitary organization had been brought here and reconstruction of the castle had been started, presumably to become future headquarters of Adolph Hitler. Russians who entered the castle found mined tunnels and shafts cut out in the basement. After the war Książ was abandoned for a few years and not until 1956 first restoration works had been started. At present the greatest admiration arouses Maximilian Hall – a two-storey chamber decorated in Vienna Baroque style.

LEGNICA

For the first time the name of Legnica appears in a written document in 1149. At the end of the 12th century under the rule of king Henry the Bearded a fortified castle became one of the first bricked strongholds in Poland. At the foot of the castle a town developed which since the 13th century became a capital of the Legnica Duchy, and later of the Legnica-Brześć Duchy. In 1241 at the outskirts of town a great battle (the Battle of Legnica) took place during Mongol invasion of Europe. In the battle Polish duke Henry the Pious of Silesia was defeated and killed.

Rapid growth of the town and castle in the 16th century made Legnica an important cultural centre in Lower Silesia. For a short period of time even a university was established here. The Thirty Years' War brought economical decline and large demographic losses due to epidemics. With the death of duke George Wilhelm, the last male descendant of Silesian Piast line in 1675, Legnica lands passed into the hands of Habsburgs. Rapid economic growth took place at the end of the 19th century but was interrupted by I and II World Wars.

Beside of the castle, in Legnica one can visit the 14th century cathedral with beautiful Gothic sculptures and epitaphs, statues of saints, bronze baptismal font ma-

de in the 13th century, Baroque altar and gravestone of princely couple Ludwik II and Elizabeth of Brandenburg (*Elżbieta Brandenburska*). Another interesting building is the former Town Hall, a group of 8 tenement houses called "herring houses" (named after fish trading on ground floor), and houses with beautiful sgrafitto decoration, i.e. "Pod Przepiórczym Koszem" house and Scultetus House (Kamienica Scultetusa).

In Legnickie Pole, a nearby village, a jewel of Baroque architecture is situated: a church and monastery of Benedictines, erected in early 18th century by abbot Othmar Zinke. The most splendid decoration of the church are frescos by Kosmas Damian Asam of Munich, presenting scenes from the history of the Order and the region.

LICHEŃ

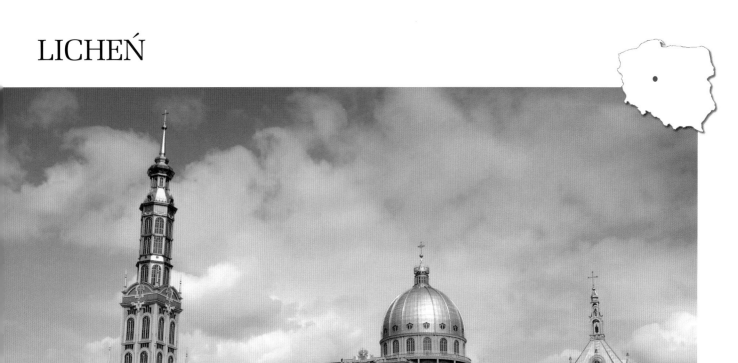

S anctuary in Licheń is one of important pilgrim's centres in Poland. Every year about 1,500,000 pilgrims and tourists come here. The history of the sanctuary dates back to 1813, when in the Battle of Leipzig, called the Battle of the Nations, a blacksmith from Licheń, Tomasz Kłossowski, fighting on the side of Napoleon, was seriously wounded. He prayed for death. Then St. Mary appeared to him, asking to find her image and bring it to his native village. Many years have passed when on one of roadside trees the healed soldier found a painting of a woman by unknown artist resembling Madonna seen on Leipzig. Kłossowski took painting with him and put it in a small shrine near Licheń. Soon rumours spread that Madonna showed up to passers-by.

In 1949 Licheń parish was taken over by Marian Fathers. In 1967 Stefan cardinal Wyszyński crowned the painting of Our Lady of Licheń. The construction of the Basilica named in honour of Our Lady of Sorrows, Queen of Poland was initiated by rev. Eugeniusz Makulski. Consecration of Basilica took place in 2004.

The church was designed by Barbara Bielecka. The Sanctuary is Poland's largest church, the eighth largest in Europe and twelveth in the world. Its length is 139 m, width 77 m, and area – 23 thousands m^2. The Basilica has got 365 windows (number of days in a year). Pilgrims enter by 52 doors and 33 steps, denoting the number of weeks per year and age of Christ, respectively. In bell-tower there is the biggest in Poland and third in Europe bell called "Maryja Bogurodzica", weighing ca. 15 tonnes. The church houses also the biggest organ in Poland consisting of 20 thousands pipes. This is the third biggest instrument in Europe.

Although the surrounding area is picturesque, Licheń is not a tourist place. It is a place of cogitation and man`s spiritual revival.

LIDZBARK WARMIŃSKI

Lidzbark Warmiński is located in north-west part of Warmian-Masurian Province on Łyna River and its tributary, the Symsarna river. In Mediaeval time tribes of Warmians and Bartians lived here, later re-settled by Teutonic Order Knights. In mid-13th century Lidzbark became a bishopric and lands ruled by bishops got the name *Warmia*. In the next century the town expanded, and was surrounded by defence walls. A gothic castle was built. At that time Lidzbark began to play the role of a principal seat of Warmia bishops transferred from Orneta. A period of prosperity for the town came to a close after wars at the beginning of the 18th century and partitions of Poland.

The most important historic monument of Lidzbark Warmiński is bishop's castle from the 14th century which is the best preserved mediaeval fortification on the area of Poland. In the 16th century the castle lost its military importance, slowly evolving into a manor. In the castle so-called "cardinal rooms" were added to the north wing and a palace in Baroque style was added to the south wing. During the Great Northern War (1700–1721) the town was the residence of king Charles XII of Sweden, who ordered to take away all pieces of art and library collec-

tions. In following years Warmia bishops attempted to restore splendour to the castle, but annexation of these lands by the Kingdom of Prussia in 1772 led to a significant decrease of church revenues and finally to downfall of bishops residence.

An important object in the town is the late Gothic parish church erected in the 14th century. Inside there are a few historic altars, a Classicistic pulpit, a Baroque baptismal font and the most precious artefact – the mediaeval herm (a bust reliquary) of St. Ida stored in the vault.

A four-storey Gothic gate called *Wysoka Brama* built in 1352 as part of fortification system of the town is very impressive. Also a wooden Orthodox church funded as Evangelical temple by the king Frederick Wilhelm III of Prussia is very interesting.

LUBLIN

On the site where Lublin castle stands today in the 10th century a wooden stronghold was erected with a surrounding borough. In the 14th century under the rules of king Casimir the Great the stronghold was disassembled and a new stone castle was built. Lublin developed the fastest in the 15th and 16th centuries taking profits of its location on a trade route connecting West Europe and the Black Sea. At that time the town was one of the most important Reformation centres in Poland.

Lublin played a significant role in the history of Poland since in 1569 a Union of Lublin was signed here uniting the Kingdom of Poland and Grand Duchy of Lithuania. In the 17th century the town declined due to wars. It was only in late 18th century when the town began develop again.

During the II world war at the outskirts of Lublin the Nazis established a concentration and extermination camp Majdanek. Now it holds a museum. After liberation in 1944 the town was a seat of the provisional communist Polish government and the main political centre of Polish communist movement.

The most important relics of Lublin is the Holy Trinity Church erected on the castle ground most probably in the 14th century. The king Władysław II Jagiełło funded beauti-

ful byzantine-ruthenian frescos decorating the interior of the Gothic chapel. Also worth seeing are remains of medieval defence walls and town gates, e.g. Krakow Gate (*Brama Krakowska*), built at first in Gothic style, and later modernized in Baroque style. Equally interesting is *Grodzka* Gate connecting the Old Town with the castle, which in the 18th century was transformed into a tenement house. An important monument is archiepiscopal see built between 1586–1604. It is one of the oldest Baroque churches outside Italy.

ŁAŃCUT THE CASTLE OF LUBOMIRSKI FAMILY

The castle of Lubomirski family had been erected by order of Stanisław Lubomirski in the years 1629- 1641 as a residence of type *palazzo fortificato*, i.e. fortified palace. Fortifications served well during Swedish Deluge (wars with Sweden), because the castle had not been conquered. In the second half of the 18th century the then owner of the palace, duchess Izabela Lubomirska, a daughter of Czartoryski, transformed it into a modern residence – one of the most magnificent noble residences in Europe. At that time the castle lost its defensive character, and gardens and game park had been added. Łańcut became an important cultural centre in Poland. On the turn of the 19th and 20th century the palace received a new façade in French neo-baroque style. Water supply network and sewage system had been installed, power plant had been built and telephone line hooked up. Palace became among the most modern European residences.

The last owner of the palace was Alfred III Potocki ranked among the world elite of establishment. During the II world war the residence had been occupied by Wehrmacht. Just before entering of Red Army Potocki successfully took away a significant part of most valuable castle collections. Most of them never came back to Poland.

Since 1944 the palace houses a museum. Despite taking away a large fraction of collections the store which remained in the palace is still very impressive. The most precious pieces of art are: *A Self-portrait* by *Sofonisby Anguissoli* of 1556 and sculpture by Antonio Canova representing Henryk Lubomirski as Cupid. In Łańcut there is the best preserved and the biggest in Poland noble library counting 22 thousand volumes. Original furnishing of palace chambers was saved as well as splendid collection of horse-drawn carriages and well preserved scenic park in English style (area of 35 ha) with several historic objects: orangery, romantic Zameczek (Little Castle), manege, stables and coach house.

MALBORK TEUTONIC CASTLE

The castle in Malbork is one of the biggest castles in mediaeval Europe. It became the seat of the Teutonic Order and Europe's largest Gothic fortress. Since 1309 it was a capital of the Monastic State of the Teutonic Knights. The castle played the role of a fortress, as well as headquarters of the Grand Master, it was also a monastery and a representative site. In the 14th century in Medium Castle a Great Refectory had been built – one of the biggest representative halls in the then Europe and magnificent Palace of the Grand Master. The huge fortress was surrounded with moats and defence walls.

During the Thirteen Years' War, in June 1457, the Polish army seized power over Malbork. In the 17th century some rooms in the Palace of Grand Masters were adapted for royal apartments. Soon after the roofs of High Castle were destroyed because of a fire. The most severe devastation the castle suffered when Prussian army garrisoned here on the turn of the 18th and 19th century.

The history of Malbork raised an interest at the beginning of the 19th century which resulted in starting restoration works. In 1816 a Malbork Castle Reconstruction Committee was formed, superior target of which was restoration of medieval character of the castle. In the eighties of the 19th century

Conrad Emanuel Steinbrecht was appointed the manager of works. He supervised the works with great reverence, being faithful to a rule: "no other step than within historical spirit". Restoration of the castle aroused interest and support of the society. During its reign Wilhelm II, German emperor, visited castle in Malbork over 30 times.

Malbork castle restoration was finished in 1931. Soon it attracted legions of tourists from Germany and the rest of Europe. There was a museum opened in the castle, richly furnished with militaries, old coins, and archaeological artefacts.

In 1997 the whole castle has won the designation of World Heritage Site from UNESCO.

MASURIAN NATURAL LANDSCAPE PARK

Masurian Natural Landscape Park is one of the largest scenic parks in Poland. It was established in 1977 to preserve natural and cultural values of the region. Its surface covers over 50,000 hectares, of which forests occupy 29,000 hectares, lakes and rivers 18,000 hectares, and remaining area consists of fields and meadows. There are several nature reserves on the area of the park. The most important is Krutynia reserve, protecting Krutyńskie Lake and upstream of Krutynia river. Canoeing trips are popular in this river because this is one of the most charming canoeing routes in Europe. From Zyndaki village to Bełdany Lake, the route is over 100 km long. Among other interesting reserves are the ornithological reserve in Łuknajno Lake or peatbog reserves (Zakręt, Królewska Sosna or Gązawa).

The Masurian Natural Landscape Park, also called the "Country of a Thousand Lakes" (*Kraina Tysiąca Jezior*) is one of the most frequently visited recreation regions in Poland. Many lakes are connected by channels, creating navigable routes used mainly by tourists.

The biggest lake both on the area of the Masurian Natural Landscape Park and all Poland is Śniardwy Lake of the area 11,416 hectares. Erratic boulders in big num-

bers deposited on the bottom make navigation difficult. There are eight isles on the lake, the largest of which being Szeroki Ostrów, Czarci Ostrów and Wyspa Pajęcza.

In the region and neighbourhood of the Masurian Natural Landscape Park one can find many interesting sites, as e.g. Hitler's headquarters in Gierłoż and the main seat of German army in Mamerki, a fortress Boyen in Giżyck, historical bridges in Stańczyki, a sanctuary in Święta Lipka, Teutonic castles in Kętrzyn, Giżycko, Reszel and Ryn as well as palaces in Sztynort, Sorkwity or Brzeźnica.

MOSZNA

The castle in Moszna is one of the most splendid noble residences in Poland and one of the best known historical monuments of Opole. It took its present shape not so long ago – on the turn of the 19th century. Earlier a small hunting palace in Baroque style stood here, which became the property of Hubert Thiele-Winckler in 1863. Due to unknown reasons the palace burned down in 1896. Right after the fire Hubert Thiele-Winckler restored the palace in its original shape, and during next several years enlarged the building by a neo-gothic representation eastern wing, probably designed by himself. In the years 1912–1914 a neo-renaissance western wing had been built. The edifice created by its owner was constructed in several significantly different architectural styles. The castle in its present shape occupies about 8000 m², it has got 365 rooms, and 99 turrets and towers.

The castle in Moszna remained in the possession of the Thiele-Winckler family until 1945, when the owners abandoned it escaping from approaching front line. For a short time Red Army soldiers and Balkan refugees stayed here, destroying the palace furnishing. Nowadays the palace houses a medical centre for neurosis treatment and private stud farm.

The palace adjoins the park of the area ca 100 ha, with no precisely determined borders. Before the war anyone could visit the park, row the boat in lakes and water pools connected by canals. In the park one can find a necropolis with remains of Thiele-Winckler family.

NIEDZICA

The castle in Niedzica is a Mediaeval stronghold picturesquely located on limestone 30 m above Czorsztyn Lake. Unusual architectural and scenic values attract many tourists every year.

The castle was erected by Kokos from Brezovica (*Kokosz Berzeviczy*) between the years 1320 and 1326 on the site of an ancient stronghold guarding trade route and Hungarian border. In the 16th century the castle became the property of Horvath family, who rebuilt it and fortified. The next century brought incessant riots in Hungary – at that time the castle had fallen into decline and finally was not suitable for dwelling. Fire of the Horvath family castle in Plavec in 1817 resulted in that Niedzica had been restored as a rural noble residence. Residential wings of lower castle and chapel had been reconstructed and a ball room had been constructed, leaving the upper castle ruined.

The last owner left Niedzica in 1943. A few years after the war the castle became the property of the Polish Minister of Culture. It has served as a historical museum ever since. A few rooms were made available for tourists.

According to a popular legend an Inca treasure is hidden in the castle. In the 18th century Sebastian Berzeviczy fell in love with the alleged Inca princess. As a result of persecutions they fled to Europe with their daughter Umina and settled at the Niedzica castle. However, Umina was assassinated and her son adopted by relatives who changed his name to Benesz. In 1946 his descendant Andrzej Benesz came to the castle, and in family archives found information about hiding place under stairs. He found there a leaden case with some "quipu" writings (used in the Inca Empire colored spun and plied thread or cotton cords with numeric and other values encoded by knots) with golden plates. Some consider quipu as indication how to find a treasure of Incas in the vicinity of the castle.

NOWY WIŚNICZ

The first owner of Wiśnicz was the family of Griffins. Later the property has been taken over by the house of Kmita, Szreniawa coat of arms, in the 14th century. Members of this family ranked among a political elite of the then Poland. They erected a Gothic castle in Wiśnicz, the first made of brick, which at that time was second to none, including Wawel, in Cracow. The residence was often visited by noble guests such as king Sigismund I the Old (*Zygmunt I Stary*), Bona Sforza d'Aragona (*queen Bona*) or king Sigismund II Augustus (*Zygmunt II August*). In the 16th century the castle passed to the hands of Count Sebastian Lubomirski. His son Stanislaw rebuilt the castle in Baroque style. At that time there were 100 rooms beautifully decorated. Floors and doors were made of precious wood species; all frames had been sculpted in marble, and windows filled with colourful stained-glass. Castle's halls were decorated with paintings by Titian, Raphael Sanzio (Raffaello) and Dürer. A collection of books formed a huge library in the castle. At the feet of the castle Lubomirski established a town which had been named Nowy Wiśnicz. In 1616 the town had been given a settlement grant, and also obtained a right to organize three fairs per year and a right to store goods imported from Hungary.

Nowy Wiśnicz was designed based on a square plan. Two main streets branched off from the market place: one leading to the castle and another to Bochnia, a town in vicinity. The town grew quickly, in part owing its development to brought-in Jewish people.

After the death of Stanislaw Lubomirski the town declined because his heirs did not consider Wiśnicz as a family head residence. Wiśnicz suffered during Swedish Deluge (wars with Sweden) and the Bar Confederation (*Konfederacja barska*). The town was severely destroyed by fire in 1863 which took a heavy toll of almost all wooden houses in town.

PIENINY MOUNTAINS

Pieniny is a 30 km long mountain range, being a very attractive tourist region in Poland. The Pieniny National Park was established in the most interesting part of the mountains since at least 50% of all animal species known in Poland can be found here. Plant cover is very diversified and rock formations are very impressive, e.g. *Trzy Korony* or *Sokolica*. Here were discovered acid mineral springs saturated with carbon dioxide, called acidic waters, which are exploited in health resorts in Szczawnica and Krościenko.

The greatest attraction of Pieniny is rafting trip in Dunajec gorges. According to a legend Bolesław I the Great contributed to the gorge origin, by cutting the rocks with his sword to make river outlet. Another legend says that the gorge appeared when snake king running away through the mountains, furrowed a crevice with his body. The route of the main rafting is 15 km long. It starts in a raft harbour in Kąty, and ends in Szczawnica or in Krościenko if water level is higher than usual. The Dunajec River makes seven loops in its gorge, passing between vertical rocks. Rafting trip lasts ca 2–3 hours, during which the tourists admire panorama of Pieniny, of the *Aksamitka* top, the likely shelter of Janosik (a local hero), *Ostra*

Skała or *Golica*, the slopes of which resemble hoods. The slopes are called Seven Monks (*Siedem Mnichów*), because according to a legend these rocks are sinful monks from nearby Red Monastery turned into stones. Rafting season lasts from April,1 until October, 31.

Also the Czorsztyn Reservoir is very attractive for tourists. On its banks a castle in Niedzica is situated and ruins of castle in Czorsztyn. Tourists often visit regional historic churches and Orthodox churches, e.g. in Grywałd or Jaworki. A church in Grywałd dates back to the 15th century. The building is of framework structure. Polychromes made in 1618 are well preserved inside as well as the altar with precious triptych painted in the 16th century. The Orthodox church in Jaworki was built at the end of the 18th century. Richly decorated iconostasis deserves particular attention.

PIESKOWA SKAŁA

Pieskowa Skała is a small settlement in the valley of river Prądnik, mentioned first time in the document of 1315. In early 14th century on the order of Polish king Casimir the Great (*Kazimierz Wielki*) a fortress was built in Pieskowa Skała as part of the defensive chain of castles protecting southern border of Poland and important trade route. According to a legend, Pieskowa Skała was granted to Piotr Szafraniec by king Wladislaw Jagiellon as a reward for faithful service and meritorious participation in the Battle of Grunwald. The castle was a residence of Szafraniec family until early 17th century. In late 15th century descendants of Piotr Szafraniec went about alchemy and robbery, and the castle served as an outing place for plundering of merchants passing by. In 1484 Krzysztof Szafraniec was sentenced to death by beheading by the order of king Wladislaw II of Poland (*Władysław Jagiellończyk*) for shade dealings unbecoming of a knight. The execution took place on Wawel Hill in Krakow.

In the late 16th century works were started to convert the castle into a Renaissance residence. It is probable that the main designer of this conversion was Italian architect Mikołaj Castiglione. In the mid-17th century the castle passed into hands of Michał Zebrzydowski, who surrounded the residence with modern fortification system. During Swedish Deluge the castle was destroyed, and later taken over by the family of Wielkopolski who restored the place in 1768.

At the turn of the 19th century the castle became a ruin. Thanks to the efforts of Adolf Dygasiński and Józef Zawadzki, the Auction Society "Pieskowa Skała Castle" bought out the ruins and restored the castle and turned it into a luxury pension.

An interesting legend is related with the name Pieskowa Skała telling of a castle owner's daughter imprisoned in starvation tower. The girl was sentenced to death for a love of squire. Supposedly her faithful dog climbed steep mountain every night bringing leftovers. Since that time the hill is called "Dog's Rock" (Pieskowa Skała).

There is a characteristic, about 25-m high, lime rock in nearby, being a symbol of Ojcow National Park. Due to its shape it is sometimes called the "Devil's Rock" (Czarcia Skała) or Sokolica, or the most often "Hercules Club" (*Maczuga Herkulesa*).

PŁOCK

At the beginning of the Polish statehood Płock was one of the more important towns in the country. Before Christianity Tumskie Hill (*Wzgórze Tumskie*) was a site of pagan worship. In 1000 Benedictine monks were brought to the town. Under the rules of king Władysław Herman and Bolesław the Wrymouth Płock played the role of the state capital. The town developed well thanks to advantageous location on the Vistula river bank which was the main trading route in Poland at that time. Płock was severely destroyed by wars with Sweden. The economic situation improved only in the 19th century. The remains of medieval defence walls were disassembled, new streets and quarters were marked out, water supply system was constructed, wooden houses were destroyed and exchanged with bricked houses.

Among the most important monuments of Płock is a cathedral basilica situated on Tumskie Hill. It was erected by the order of bishop Alexander from Malonne between the years 1130–1144. There are many historic tombstones and altars inside. Royal chapel holds a sarcophagus of Władysław Herman and of Bolesław the Wrymouth. Another interesting object, unique in Poland, is Old Catholic church of Mariavites built in neo-Gothic style at the beginning of the 20th century. In its basement Feliksa Kozłowska, a mariavitism founder, is buried. On the town market square a Classicistic town hall is situated built in the years 1824–1827 according to a design of Jakub Kubicki. Everyday on the tower appear statues of natural size showing knighting of the Bolesław's knights and a bugle-call is played everyday.

POZNAŃ

Considered a cradle of Polish statehood Poznań is a hypothetical place of baptism of Mieszko I of Poland. In 968 the first Poland's bishop, Jordan, established a seat here, and until destruction of the town by Bohemian king Bretislaus I in 1039, Poznań played the role of a capital of the state.

The city developed well thanks to advantageous location on trade route from Germany to Little Poland (*Małopolska*) and to Lithuania. The town prospered the best in the 16th and early 17th centuries. Swedish Deluge and the wars resulted in destruction and plundering of Poznań. During partitions of Poland Poznań passed again under rules of Prussia and was incorporated in Poland only after Poland regained independence in 1918.

There are many historic monuments in Poznań, dating back to origins of the Polish state and other periods. The oldest in Poland cathedral was erected on the site of early Romanesque church from the late 10th century. The cathedral is an exceptional place because its is a burial place of first Polish rulers: Mieszko I, Bolesław the Wrymouth, Mieszko II, Casimir I the Restorer, Władysław Odonic, Przemysł I, Bolesław the Pious and Przemysł II.

On the Old Town market square a beautiful town hall is situated, considered a pearl of Renaissance architecture. The building has splendid richly decorated facade. There are shown allegories of virtues, medallions with busts of ancient personages, and rulers of Poland from Jagiellon dynasty. The town hall is crowned with a clock tower and a "jester's device" where at noon a pair of billy goats appear. Inside there are a few beautifully ornamented halls, e.g. the Great Hall (*Sala Wielka*), once being a room in which proceedings of city court of justice were held, the Royal Hall (*Sala Królewska*) – a room of city council and the Courtroom (*Sala Sądowa*).

Another precious historic monument of Poznań is former Jesuits College and collegiate church erected in the 17th century with richly decorated façade. Inside one can find beautiful polychromies, altar and organ made by the best organ maker in the late 19th century, Friedrich Ladegast.

HEL PENINSULA

el Peninsula, which separates the Baltic Sea from the Bay of Gdansk, is one of the most interesting landscape and nature peculiarities in Poland. It is about 35 km long, and its width varies from approximately 200 m at its starting point to over 3 km near its tip, the town of Hel. On the 17th century map the peninsula was a chain of islands that formed a strip of land only during summer due to the effects of sea current.

Typical feature of Hel Peninsula is its microclimate. Here winds are blowing the strongest, precipitation is the smallest and number of sunny days per year is the highest. As a result of particular landscape and natural conditions the whole Peninsula belongs to the Seaside Scenic Park since 1978.

Hel is the only town in Poland located so far in the sea. There are about 5 thousands inhabitants living in this farthest point of Peninsula. Hel settlement was established in mediaeval times but it was located in a different place. According to a legend, former Hel sunk in the Baltic waters for sins of its inhabitants who dealt with piracy. At present Hel is a holiday resort and fishing locality. A museum of fishing has a seat here – the only open air ethnographical museum of folk fishing boats in Poland. Near sea station of the Gdansk University there is a seal aquarium, and a lighthouse at the outskirts of town. The lighthouse is accessible for visitors – there is a splendid view giving on the Peninsula, the Bay of Gdansk and Baltic Sea.

Hel Peninsula is also a wonderful place for fortifications lovers. It was turned into a fortified region. Many historical military objects built before and during the war, e.g. the heaviest Polish artillery waterfront battery from the time of September Campaign of 1939, today are open to tourists.

PRZEMYŚL

Przemyśl is the oldest borough on the eastern fringe of Poland, picturesquely located in the valley of San river. It belonged to Grody Czerwieńskie, a border region between Poland and Kievan Russ, being the subject of rivalry between Poland, Hungary and Russia. According to a legend town's name is derived from the name of its founder – a Lechite duke Przemysł.

It is assumed that Christianity came to this land very early. Archeological remains testify to the presence of a monastic settlement on the Castle Hill as early as the 9th century. At that time presumably, Przemyśl was a local centre for propagation of Christianity, spread to nearby lands.

In the 14th century a stone castle was raised on the hill. The town developed well until mid-17th century, becoming one of the important cultural and economic centres of the then Poland. Like nearby Lvov, the city's population consisted of a great number of nationalities, including Ukrainians, Poles, Jews, Germans, Czechs and Armenians. In the 17th century the wars destroyed Przemyśl. As a result of partitions of Poland the town was incorporated into the Austrian Empire. In mid-19th century the Austrians built their fortifications on nearby hills, transforming Przemyśl into a fortress, third in size in Europe. It played a significant role during the I world war.

The most valuable historic monuments of Przemyśl are the remains of early mediaeval Christian structures on the Castle Hill, where a stone castle was erected later on, an archiepiscopal basilica, under floor of which traces of Romanesque rotunda were found, a monastery, a Franciscan church with relics of St. Vincent, and town's market place.

An interesting object situated outside the town's centre is Tartar's mound, called Przemysław Mound. Neither the date of its raising, nor the aim is known. Some historians assume that this is a grave of Tartars who died during the raids, others assume it a tomb of town's founder, duke Przemysł.

RADRUŻ

Radruż is a small village located near the Ukrainian border in Subcarpathian Province. For the first time Radruż was mentioned in records made in mid-15th century. The inhabitants were mainly farmers, who raised sheep and kept bees. In the 16th century the land was invaded by Tartars many times. As a result of attack in 1531 an Orthodox church was destroyed; however, some time later a new church was erected in the same place. St.Paraskewa church most probably was funded by Jan Płaza, a Lubaczów starost. At present the church belongs to the most valuable examples of wooden sacral architecture in Poland. Late Gothic Orthodox church in Radruż is a defensive structure, and was built as a framework construction of fir and oak wood. Inside one can admire original polychromes made in 1648. Part of historic furnishings of the church was moved and incorporated into collections in Łańcut, Lvov and Lubaczów.

The historic complex in Radruż includes the Orthodox church, wooden bell tower and bricked mortuary called Seminarian House (*Dom Diaka*). The whole complex is surrounded by a stone wall covered with shingle roofing.

Close to the Orthodox church are situated small cemeteries with a few relics of graves and a tombstone of Katarzyna Dubniewiczowa of 1682. There is a legend connected to the Dubniewicz family saying that during Tartar's attack in 1672 Maria, a beautiful daughter of Katarzyna Dubniewicz, surrendered to Tartars in return for a promise to save people and the church. She was sold to Constantinople, where one of Turkish officials fell in love with her. After 27 years of captivity Dubniewicz's daughter managed to come back to Radruż with considerable fortune, which she donated to the church to show gratitude for home-coming. Presumably she was buried in the restored church after her death at the beginning of the 18th century.

ROGALIN THE RACZYŃSKI PALACE

For the first time Rogalin was mentioned in historical records in 1294 as a property of Łodzia family. In the 16th century Rogalin manor belonged to Arciszewski house. Here Krzysztof Arciszewski, one of the most famous Polish explorers and adventurers, was born, the admiral of Dutch fleet and general of artillery for the king Władysław IV Vasa. In the second half of the 18th century Rogalin became the property of Raczyński family and remained in their hands until 1939.

The palace in Rogalin was planned with impressive proportions, to be a representative place of residence showing social status of the whole family line. The works started in 1768. The building had been designed in late baroque style by unknown architect. Shortly after completing the works modernization of the palace in Classicistic style had been commissioned to architects of Stanisław August Poniatowski – Dominik Merlini and Jan Chrystian Kamsetzer.

Main body frontage of the palace is decorated with Raczyński coat of arms. By means of arch galleries the palace is connected to annexes perpendicular to it. Three courtyards lead to the residence. Family residence in Rogalin is surrounded by a beautiful park of the area of 37 ha established in the second half of the 18th century. A Baroque French-style garden adjoining the palace is one of the best preserved gardens of this type in Poland. Purposely planted and pruned hedges create a labyrinth of paths. In various parts of the park numerous sculptures represent mythological figures.

More distant fragment of the park was designed in English style. It opens into wide meadows of the Scenic Park of Wielkopolska and the most famous local oak trees named: Lech, Czech and Rus. As the legend says, centuries ago three brothers parted here and each of them got on his own road, finally establishing a new state for each brother: Poland, Bohemia and Russia, respectively.

RZESZÓW

Rzeszów was granted municipal rights and charters enabling its fast development in the 14th century. A period of the highest splendour fell on the turn of the 16th century, when Mikołaj Spytko Ligęza was the owner of the town. He fortified the town, funded many buildings and churches and started to construct a castle. In 1638 Rzeszów passed into hands of Lubomirski family who set up here a famous college of Piarists (the *Order of Poor Clerks Regular of the Mother of God of the Pious Schools*; a Catholic educational order). In late 17th century the town declined due to wars, fires and bad administration. Economic development was back in mid-19th century, but only becoming a capital of the province after II world war made Rzeszów a real cultural and administrative centre of the south-eastern Poland.

There are about 400 historic buildings in the town, among them the most precious is parish church from the 15th century and Bernardine monastic complex housing also a mausoleum of Ligęza family, the founders of monastery and owners of Rzeszów. Baroque interior of the church, from the 18th century, is of particular interest.

In the centre of the Old Town there is a market place with some beautiful tenement houses and imposing town hall, which origins date back to the 16th century. One of the most characteristic monuments of Rzeszów is a castle situated to the south of the market place. It was built in *palazzo fortezza* style. It was modernized many times, among the others, by a famous architect Tylman van Gameren. Mikołaj Spytko Ligęza was a founder and first owner of the castle. Then the castle passed into hands of Lubomirski family, who kept the castle until 1820, when the castle had been sold to Austrian authorities. From that time on there was a prison in the castle. In late 19th century the building was in very poor condition. Renewal was ineffective so most of walls were disassembled and the structure restored. Nowadays the castle houses a court of justice, Museum of Justice and some cultural events take place there.

SANDOMIERZ

Gallus Anonymus (*Gall Anonim*) in his *Chronicles and Deeds of the Dukes or Princes of the Poles*, ca. 1115, counts Sandomierz as well as Krakow and Wrocław as the most important and the oldest towns in Poland. First mentions of Sandomierz date back to the 11th century, although the settlement is much older. The town importance was confirmed in the last will of king Bolesław the Wrymouth, because Sandomierz became a capital of provincial Duchy granted to Henry of Sandomierz. The province was later ruled by Casimir II the Just and Leszek the White. The economic growth of the town occurred in the 14th century thanks to privileges granted by Casimir the Great. Prosperity of the town came to a close in the 17th century (wars with Sweden) and it was not until the twenties and thirties of the 20th century and post-war period when Sandomierz started to develop again.

In Sandomierz there are over 120 historic buildings erected in various periods of time. The most interesting is a town hall erected in the 14th century and rebuilt two centuries later. Its layout is square, it is crowned with an attic and is considered one of the most beautiful Renaissance town halls in Poland. Another important historic building is a cathedral erected in the 14th century in place of a Romanesque church destroyed during Tartar's invasions. Inside there are polychromes of the 15th century, original marble altars, and in a cathedral's treasure – relics of the wood of the Holy Cross, donated to the town by king Władysław Jagiełło for merits of Sandomierz knighthood in the Battle of Grunwald. Not so far from the market place one can find a town gate, one of best preserved in Poland, so called Opatów Gate (*Brama Opatowska*). It was built in the 14th century as one of the four entrance gates to the town. In the 16th century it was heightened and crowned with Renaissance attic. To the south of the Old Town there is a castle built on a hill in place of an old wooden borough. Until wars with Sweden the castle had four wings. Only one wing remained until these days.

SŁOWIŃSKI NATIONAL PARK

Słowiński National Park was established in 1967 to preserve in unchanged form a system of coastal lakes, forests, peat bogs and, most of all, a unique sand bar with migrating sand dunes. Park owns its name to the Slavic tribe of Slowincy, who used to live in this swampy, difficult to reach area. At the village of Kluki there is an open air museum in which several aspects of their everyday life and culture are presented.

About 80% of the Park surface are water and wetlands; therefore, this area is a bird hatchery for many species (257 species). Lakes of the Park appeared as a result of closing the bay with sand deposited by sea currents and winds. Nowadays, shallow lakes are fed by fresh water from nearby rivers. The biggest is the Łebsko lake, third biggest lake in Poland. Forests (mainly pines) cover 80% of wooded areas.

The most known feature of the Słowiński National Park is migrating dunes, which appeared as a consequence of forest cutting. After cutting out trees dunes deprived of natural protection started to migrate inland due to blowing western and northern winds. Sand particles move forward when wind blows with the speed at least 5 m per second; therefore, migration is fastest in autumn and winter. Dune motion varies and depends on site and land formation. The slowest dunes (ca 3 m per year) migrate in the eastern and western part of the Park, while the quickest (10 m per year) in the middle part of the spit. The highest dune called Łącka Góra is 45 m high. The biggest peak of the Park - Rowokol (115 meters above sea level) is also an excellent observation point.

Europe's biggest migrating dunes, the unique feature of the Słowiński National Park, has become a part of UNESCO World Biosphere Reserve in 1977.

SOPOT

First mentions of Sopot date back to the 13th century. At that time Sopot was only a small village earning living of fishery. During Renaissance times it became quite popular resting site for rich Gdańsk burghers. At the end of the 18th century count Kajetan Sierakowski built here the first summer house, but not earlier than thanks to the activity of Jan Jerzy Haffner, a former medic of Napoleonic army, Sopot transformed into a popular summer resort. Haffner financed a Bath House facility (first in Sopot). In the following years Haffner erected more facilities. By 1824 a sanatorium was opened to the public, as well as a wooden pier, cloakrooms, and a park. Local salines applied in treatment of locomotive organs diseases and rheumatic pains, attracted many patients from Gdańsk, and later from more distant parts of the country, transforming Sopot into one of the most popular holiday resorts at the Baltic coast. The new casino became one of the main sources of income for the town. After II world war it was renamed as the Grand Hotel and continues to be one of the most luxurious hotels in Poland. After the II world war Sopot became a part of the Tricity (Trójmiasto), preserving its recreational and service character.

The most known facility in Sopot is the Europe's longest pier made of wood. It is 512 m long out of which 458 m enters the Gdańsk Bay. First pier was built by Jerzy Haffner in 1829 and was 41 m long. At first it served as a quay but with the passing of time it transformed into a recreation facility.

As a consequence of many cultural events Sopot is sometimes called a town of artists. Numerous festivals take place here as well as cyclic shows, i.e. Sopot Festival, "Number one" Festival, Kaleidoscope of Music Forms, "Two Theatres" Festival, Sopot Molo Jazz Festival, Mundus Cantat or TOP Trendy Festival.

STAŃCZYKI AQUEDUCTS IN ROMINCKA FOREST

Stańczyki is a small village in north-eastern Poland, located on the area sometimes called Mazury Garbate (Humped Masuria), hilly terrain formed by retreating glacier. Even though this is a picturesque landscape with deep gorges hiding small streams on the bottom and clean lakes this remote part of the country is seldom visited.

In a short distance to Stańczyki, so-called Aqueducts of the Romincka Forest are located, impressive railway bridges passing over the river Błędzianka. Aqueducts are the part of a railway line Gołdap-Żytkiejmy built at the beginning of the 20th century. Due to strategic reasons two bridges pass over the river valley. One served transport purposes, and second was a stand-by track in case the first bridge would be destroyed. Northern bridge had been built in the years 1912–1914, and southern in the years 1923–1926. Aqueducts are 36 m high, and 180 m long. Bridge structure is perfectly proportional. Bridge piers are carefully shaped, and classic spans joining the piers are crowned with barriers extending along the whole aqueduct length. The structure viewed from a distance reminds of Roman aqueducts.

Trains run this railway line until 1945. After the second world war Russians took apart the rail tracks. At present the bridges become a tourist attraction, still being a piece of art of civil engineering.

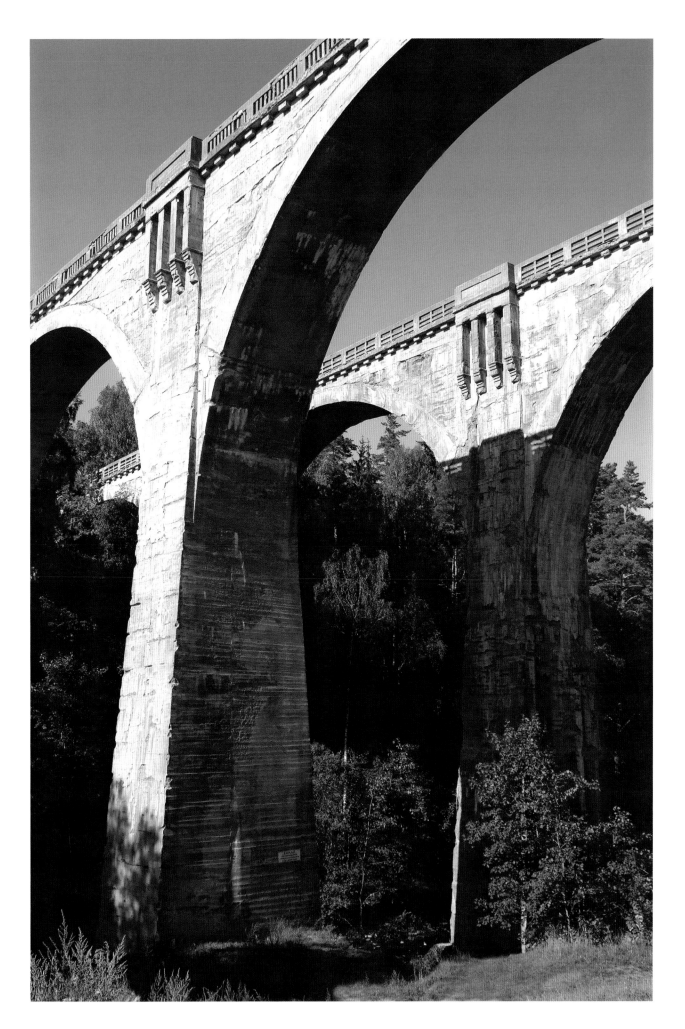

SUWAŁKI SCENIC PARK

The Suwałki Scenic Park covers an area of over 6000 ha. It was established in 1976 as the first scenic park in Poland. Landscape formation reveals large changes in elevation rarely seen in north-eastern part of the country. The region was formed by retreating continental glacier, which left typical morainic plateau, i.e. Szurpił, Krzemianki or Dzierwan, as well as deep river valleys.

In early mediaeval times a culture of Yotvingians was in full blossom here with tribal centre on Góra Zamkowa. This was afforested country. In the 16th century a development and colonisation of local forests started. First mills and settlements of woodcutters and pitch burners were established. Further growth continued in the 18th century thanks to Camaldolese monks from Wigry monastery and protection by royal undertreasurer Antoni Tyzenhaus.

The Suwałki Scenic Park is one of the coolest regions in the country. Here winters are chilly and nearly twice as long as in south-western part of Poland. Vegetation period lasts only 180 days.

On the area of Park situated in Neman River basin (*Niemen* River) there are 22 lakes of area exceeding 1 ha. One of the largest is the Hańcza Lake, the cleanest and deepest (108.5 m) in Poland. About 24 fish species inhabit the lake including some very seldom found, e.g. Alpine bullhead (*Cottus poecilopus*) or Eurasian minnow (*Phoxinus phoxinus*).

Interesting geological reserves called boulder' fields are found in the Park. The biggest are: Głazowisko Łopuchowskie and Głazowisko Bachanowo on the Czarna Hańcza River. The fields are full of erratic boulders of different size, which number is estimated to ca 10,000 and a periphery of the biggest boulders is nearly 8 m.

SZCZECIN

O n Claudius Ptolemy's map of the 2nd century AD
a village called Susudata can be found in Szczecin
nearby. However, it is not known if it was the same site where
Mediaeval stronghold with a borough and harbour was built.

Szczecin was granted municipal rights in 1243. In the
14th century on the place of Slavic stronghold a stone castle was erected called the Pomeranian Dukes' Castle. For
centuries the town was a cultural, administrative and commercial centre of the northern part of Pomerania. The fastest growth of Szczecin took place in the 19th century and
at the beginning of the 20th century. The town became an
important industrial centre. During II world war it was destroyed seriously due to bombing by allied armies.

Worth visiting is the Pomeranian Dukes' Castle rebuilt
after war destruction and *Wały Chrobrego. Wały Chrobrego* (*Chrobry* terraces or *Hakenterrasse* in German) is
a viewing terrace 19 m above the Oder River with beautifully designed architectural complex. Province authorities,
Szczecin Maritime University, Modern Theatre (Polish
Teatr Współczesny) and National Museum have their seats here. Particular attention should be paid to Cathedral
Basilica of St. James the Apostle, constructed from the
13th to 16th century, in which one can find precious Gothic

tombstones and altars. Also Baroque Royal Gate is worth seeing, built in the years 1725–1727, decorated with many sculptures such as an eagle (Prussian emblem) and Frederick Wilhelm's initials. Other historic monuments are: Gothic Old Town Hall (later rebuilt in Baroque style), Romanesque Tower of Seven Coats (*Baszta Siedmiu Płaszczy*), tenement house of merchant Loitz family, palace *Pod Głowami* or neo-Baroque palace *Pod Globusem*, in which Princess Sophie Marie Dorothea Auguste Louise of Wurttemberg, was born in 1759, the second wife of Tsar Paul I of Russia and mother of Tsar Alexander I and Tsar Nicholas I of Russia.

EAGLE NESTS TRAIL

Eagle Nests Trail (*Szlak Orlich Gniazd*) is one of the most popular tourist trail in Poland. It spreads for a few dozens of kilometres between Krakow and Częstochowa. The trail took its name after picturesque ruins of several castles built on limestone.

The castles of *Jura Krakowsko-Częstochowska* (Krakow-Częstochowa Upland) were built in the 14th century by king Casimir the Great. They were to guard the borders of the Polish Kingdom and to protect trade route from Great Poland (*Wielkopolska*) to Krakow and further to Russ. Most of the strongholds were destroyed due to wars taking place in the 17th century.

The largest castle on the trail is a castle in Ogrodzieniec. Directly behind its gate there is a large homesteads with ruins of stables. The castle in Ogrodzieniec had several storeys and underground chambers. Its best prosperity fell in the 16th century, when the Medieval fortress was changed to a Renaissance residence. The rooms were decorated with arrases and mahogany furniture, and the castle itself was called "Small Wawel". Another object worth visiting is a stronghold in Ojców. Not much is preserved; only a gate, a tower,

a well and remains of walls. The castle was only a fortress, as shown by its location on a high hill and the thickness of walls (ca 1.5 m). The name "Ojców" was given to commemorate the father of Casimir the Great, Władysław the Small. Also attractive is the castle in Olsztyn, erected presumably on place of a former wooden stronghold. Today only fragments of walls remained and 20-m high tower.

ŚWIDNICA

The name "Świdnica" is derivative of word "svida" meaning a scrub growing once in neighbourhood of the old borough. A precise date of granting municipal rights is not known; however, as far as one can tell, it was granted in the 13th century when Świdnica was a capital of an independent Duchy of Świdnica and Jawor. In the 14th century it was second in rank biggest town in Silesia after Wrocław. At the end of the 14th century it passed under rules of Bohemian kings, in the 16th century of Habsburg family, and since 1741 it passed in Prussia hands.

The most important monument of Świdnica is a church of the peace. These churches were built by the Evangelicals with the consent of catholic Ferdinand III, Holy Roman Emperor of Habsburg house. Temple building permit was a sign of religious tolerance after wars in the 17th century. Churches of the Peace had to be built outside the city walls and made of wood with no nails or constructed of other perishable materials (sand, clay, straw) without bell-tower. Construction time could not exceed one year. The church was to served as many people as possible, therefore this temple has an area 1090 m² inside and can seat ca. 7500 persons. From three Evangelical churches which were built in Silesia only two survived until modern times – in Jawor and Świdnica. In 2001 the Church of Peace in Świdnica was listed as the UNESCO World Heritage Site.

Another very interesting town building is a Gothic cathedral erected in the 14th century by the order of duke Bolko I of Świdnica. The construction continued over 150 years. It is the largest church in Lower Silesia: the nave is 71 m long and 25 m high. The Baroque decoration dates back to the turn of the 17th century. The tower beside the church is the highest in Silesia (103 m high), and third in Poland (after Licheń and Częstochowa).

In the centre of the town a town hall, historic statues and nearby beautiful houses arrest tourist attention. At present intensive renovation works take place to restore the square market former character.

ŚWIĘTA LIPKA CZĘSTOCHOWA OF THE NORTH

The origins of the Sanctuary of St. Mary in Świę-ta Lipka date back to the 14th century. According to a legend St. Mary appeared to a prisoner sentenced to death in the night before execution, leaving a piece of wood and chisel. A convict carved a beautiful figurine of Madonna, which beauty delighted the judges. They regarded the figure as a sign from God and granted a pardon to a convict. The released prisoner got on the road to seek a big linden tree, to hang the figurine. He found a tree in the place where a basilica stands nowadays. Soon this place became famous because of miraculous restoration to health and began attract more and more pilgrims. There were among them Sigismund III Vasa, Władysław IV, John II Casimir and John III Sobieski. There were attempts to move Madonna to Kętrzyn several times, but each time the figurine miraculously came back to the linden tree.

Sometimes called "Częstochowa of the North" Święta Lipka is considered the most splendid example of late Baroque in Poland. In 1688 a monastic complex was built, including St. Mary Visitation church, cloister and Jesuit monks' house. Rich decoration is preserved in perfect condition, including sculptures, frescos, paintings, golden pieces of art and metal craftworks, e.g. magnificent Baroque gate from early 18th century.

Basilica houses an adored painting of St. Mary of Święta Lipka brought from Vilnius showing St. Mary with Infant Jesus. Particular attention should be paid to historic organ made by organ master from Kaliningrad Jan Josue Mosengel in 1721. The instrument is decorated with angels playing different instruments. Their statues as well as bells and stars placed on organ turrets are set in motion during playing the organ.

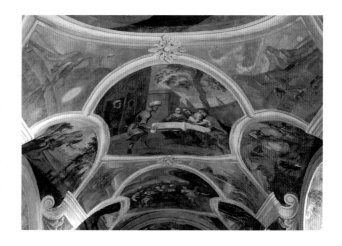

TARNÓW

Tarnów was granted municipal rights in 1330. The town owner was Spycimir Leliwita, a Krakow province governor and castellan being second in rank after king in the state. For a long time Tarnów remained in private hands and in the 15th century it became the property of Tarnowski family, descendants of Spycimir. The fastest development of the town occurred in the 16th century thanks to Jan Amor Tarnowski, Field Marshal of the Crown, who extended a defensive system of the town and granted suitable charters to merchants and craftsmen contributing to Tarnów prosperity. In the 16th century there was a school, Calvinistic church and synagogue in the town. In mid 17th century the town declined due to wars. In the second half of the 19th century thanks to railway connection with Krakow Tarnów developed well again.

Among the most important relics of the town is a Gothic town hall erected in the 14th century. Two centuries later the town was rebuilt in Renaissance style by Italian architect Gianmaria (*Jan Maria*) Mosca from Padua, called Padovano. A beautiful attic with mascaron was added at that time. In 28 attic cavities portraits of the Tarnowski family were painted; however, they did not survived until modern times. Another important relic is a cathedral with graves of Tarnowski and Ostrogski families, being the illustrious pieces of Renaissance art in Poland and Europe. Almost 14 m high, one-storey statue of Jan and Krzysztof Tarnowski is considered the most monumental Renaissance tombstone. Interesting and valuable relic of Tarnów is a bimah, i.e. the central part of the oldest in town synagogue, serving to religious ceremonies and reading of the Torah.

TATARIAN TRAIL

Bohoniki and Kruszyniany are two small villages in Podlasie Province. They are the oldest Polish centres of Muslim believers. According to a legend the nearby grounds were granted to soldiers of Tatarian units in return for saving the life of Polish king John III Sobieski (Jan III Sobieski) in the Battle of Parkany in 1683.

With the passage of time, Tatarian community assimilated with Poles, Belarusians and Lithuanians inhabiting these lands. Today there are about 4000 people of Tatarian origin. Tatars assimilated Polish language, remaining faithful to Muslim traditions and faith. Thanks to limited contacts with other Muslim believers Tatarian faith was subject to transformation only a little. One can find there pre-Muslim elements and taken-over Christian components. In Bohoniki and Kruszyniany there are mosques where Muslim holidays, i.e. Ramadan Bajram, Kurban Bajram, Ashura and Mawlid an-Nabi (Mewlud) are celebrated.

Near mosques in Bohoniki and Kruszyniany there are mizars, Muslim cemeteries (miary). The oldest tombstones date back to the 18th century. The cemeteries prove polonization of Tatars, and at the same time certify a strong need to preserve their own identity. Tombstones are decorated with crescent and inscriptions rarely used by Muslims. Cemetery in Bohoniki is one of the most important working necropoleis of Tatars in Poland.

Only few people know that the Poles owe the uhlan's tradition to Tatars. The name itself comes from Mongolian or Tatar words *oglan* or *uhuan* meaning *brave warrior*. Uhlan was a name of young men of Tatar princely families. At the turn of the 16th century a Tatar unit called "uhlan's" regiment was created in Lithuania which later gave name to famous Polish military units.

TATRA MOUNTAINS

Tatra Mountains is the highest mountain range in the Carpathians. The area covers 785 km², of which only 25% belongs to Poland. The highest top is Gerlach in Slovakia, of height 2655 m a.s.l., while the highest Polish Tatra peak is Rysy – 2499 m a.s.l.

In geological terms Tatra Mountains is young formation. The landscape is a result of glacier activity and erosion. There are about 200 lakes, mainly of postglacial origin, of which the largest is Morskie Oko Lake ("Eye of the Sea") of area 34.5 ha.

Tatra climate resembles that of Alpine region. Its characteristic feature is large variations of temperature during daytime, sudden changes of weather and high cloudiness. A frequent feature is windstorm in spring and autumn, called "halny".

The biggest town at the foot of Tatra Mountains is Zakopane, sometimes called the Winter Capital of Poland. It is the town located at the highest elevation (800–1000 m) above sea level, compared to any town in Poland. It is inhabited by about 30,000 people, being a wonderful accommodation base for hundreds of thousand of tourists in a year.

Tatra Mountains is the most difficult and dangerous mountain range in Poland. First precursors of mountaineering appeared in the 16th century. The true expansion of tourism exploded in late 19th century due to a significant group of intellectuals who settled in Zakopane delighted by the beauty of landscape and local folklore. In order to further Tatra Mountains and to help develop the region, the Tatra Society (Towarzystwo Tatrzańskie) has been set up in 1873. Thanks to activity of this Society Zakopane developed well, new mountain trails were established and many mountain lodges were built.

TATRA MOUNTAINS THE VALLEY OF THE FIVE POLISH LAKES

The Valley of the Five Polish Lakes (*Dolina Pięciu Stawów Polskich*) is one of the most valuable areas of Tatra National Park. It is a branch of the most picturesque and longest Tatra valley - the Valley of Białka. The Valley of Five Lakes is ca 4 km long and occupies an area of 6.5 km². There are a few postglacial ponds from which the valley took its name. Their total area is 61 ha. The biggest of five ponds, the Great Polish Lake (*Wielki Staw Polski*), is 1 km long, located at the height 1665 m asl. Its depth is nearly 80 m, which makes it belong to the deepest lakes in Poland.

Great Lake (*Wielki Staw*) gives a beginning to the *Roztoka* stream, which goes over the cliff that in turn forms a waterfall *Siklawa* (the biggest waterfall in Poland), ca. 70 m of height.

In the Valley of the Five Lakes there is a shelter, situated the highest in the Polish part of the Tatra Mountains. It is the only Polish Tatra shelter not accessible by car. The present shelter is a fifth in turn building erected in the Valley. The first one was established in 1876 on the initiative of Tatra Mountains Association (*Towarzystwo Tatrzańskie*). At late 19th century it was decided to construct a subsequent shelter of higher standard. Contemporary shelter was built in 1954. It is a stony wooden building

harmoniously incorporated into surrounding landscape. Due to its location it becomes a splendid base for various Tatra trails. The routes take to *Morskie Oko* through *Świstówka* and a pass of *Szpiglasowa Przełęcz*, to a shelter in *Roztoka* through a waterfall *Wodogrzmoty Mickiewicza*, to a pasture *Hala Gąsienicowa* through *Zawrat*, a pass of *Kozia Przełęcz* or *Przełęcz Krzyżne*, to *Kozi Wierch* or to a trail *Orla Perć*.

TCZEW BRIDGES

In the 13th century Tczew was a capital of Duchy ruled by Sambor II. In 1258 the first in Poland Municipal Council was set up here, earlier than similar councils in Krakow or Wrocław. It is worth noticing that the council was set up even before the town foundation (1260). Thanks to trade route and customs house on the Vistula River the town grew well, competing with Toruń and Gdańsk. Local harbour housed ships of western merchants and there was local mint in town. Tczew was destroyed by fire in 1577. For a long time the town was in decline and only establishing a railway connection between Berlin and Kaliningrad in the 19th century helped to animate the town.

The result of railway construction was building one of the most interesting historic technical monuments in Poland, a 6-span openwork bridge over the Vistula River. A cornerstone for construction was bricked by Frederick Wilhelm IV in 1857. At that time the bridge in Tczew was the longest bridge in Europe (837 m). Each pillar covered with carved stone, was crowned with two towers built in neo-Gothic style according a design of Friedrich August Stuler. Carl Lentze was an engineer responsible for the whole structure. In the years 1888–1890 due to increased traffic, second railway bridge was built in the

distance of only a few dozens of metres, while the first was changed to a road bridge. In 1912 both bridges were made longer by about 250 m to the east, as a consequence of shifting river levees.

During the II world war both bridges were important strategically; therefore, they were blown out in the first day of war, stopping redeployment of German armies. Bridges were rebuilt in the sixties of the 20th century, however, their full charm was not restored. *American Society of Civil Engineers (Amerykańskie Stowarzyszenie Inżynierów Budownictwa (ASCE))* considered the bridge in Tczew as international civil engineering masterpiece.

TORUŃ

Toruń is a town with the second highest number of Gothic relics after Krakow, representing the most important achievements of European Medieval brick architecture. Preserved houses dated back to the first centuries of the town existence are examples of the best preserved residential architecture complex in this part of Europe. The above mentioned features and almost unchanged spatial plan of the town made Old Town in Toruń to enter the UNESCO World Heritage List in 1997.

Toruń was established by Teutonic Order monks at the beginning of the 13th century. The town developed marvellously, being the main centre for crop trade between south-eastern and north-western Europe. The commerce left visible traces in municipal architecture in the form of many granaries. Soon commercial role of Toruń decreased due to Gdańsk development. After a short time of economic downfall in 1500, Toruń gained the right to construct a bridge on the Vistula river. At that time big fairs were the site of exchange of goods. Thanks to easy and dry crossing of the river the town again was being visited by merchants from the whole Europe.

The most important personality of Toruń is Nicolas Copernicus who was born here. Up to this day a 15th century Copernicus house is situated in Kopernika Street, 15.

Toruń is famous of its gingerbreads. Tradition of gingerbread baking dates back to the Medieval times. The recipe was diligently guarded secret by bakers. The greatest reputation gained a gingerbread (ca 2 m long) prepared in 1778 for tsarist Catherine I the Great.

TYKOCIN

Tykocin is a small but very charming town on the river Narew. It represents the oldest and the most beautiful urban complex of Podlasie region. Tykocin was first mentioned as a frontier stronghold in the 10th century. In the 16th century king Sigismund I the Old (*Zygmunt I Stary*) enlarged the castle erected by previous owners, transforming it into a biggest lowland fortress in Poland at that time. The castle had been abandoned after a fire in 1734. At present a private owner conducts reconstruction works.

After Swedish Deluge Stefan Czarniecki was granted Tykocin together with nearby grounds for his merits for the country. The next in turn owner of Tykocin was the family of Branicki. At that time Tykocin started to raise from decline, soon becoming the "pearl of Polish Baroque". In the years 1740–1750 thanks to Jan Klemens Branicki foundation on the main square of the town the Most Holy Trinity church had been erected. Preserved since the year 1750 confessionals, altars, baptismal font and pulpit can be seen inside. Wall polychromes decorating the interior were painted by Sebastian Eckstein in 1749, and pipe organ still in operation was constructed in 1760.

In 1522 Jewish population had been brought into Tykocin. In 1642 a bricked synagogue was built, considered the second biggest (next to Krakow synagogue) and the most important synagogue in Poland. At present a museum houses artefacts of Jewish culture and tokens of Tykocin splendour. Jewish cemetery preserved in nearby is the oldest monument of this kind in Poland.

Tykocin earned a name as a foundation site of the most important Polish order – The Order of the White Eagle (*Order Orła Białego*) which is Poland's highest decoration awarded both to civilians and the military for their merits. It was officially instituted on November 1, 1705 by king Augustus II the Strong.

WAMBIERZYCE SILESIAN JERUSALEM

According to the 13th century legend under a linden tree growing in the place where Wambierzyce Basilica stands at present, blind Jan from Raszewo regained his sight. Saint Mary with Infant Jesus with burning cross above her head showed up to him. The message about the miracle got around very fast, resulting in arrival of pilgrims and growth of Marian worship.

In the 13th century on the site of miraculous event a wooden chapel was built. In 1677 the then owner of Wambierzyce, Daniel von Osterberg, started construction of a church and the Way of the Cross. However, this church had been disassembled due to structural errors. Next owner of Wambierzyce, count von Götzen built a Baroque-style sanctuary in the years 1715–1720 and enlarged Calvary. Nowadays it counts almost 80 chapels, 12 gates and many more smaller chapels. On the turn of the 19th and 20th century nearly all chapels had been decorated with naturalistically painted wooden sculptures.

Proportions of the Visitation church façade correspond to those of Salomon temple in Jerusalem; the façade is 50 m long and 45 m high. In 1724 stairs in front of the façade were completed, in total 57 steps. This number is a sum of numbers indicating choirs of angels (9), Christ's age at crucifixion (33 years) and Mary's age at Immaculate Conception (15 years). Wambierzyce town in various ways refers to the Bible, e.g. Cedron is the name of a stream flowing by the village, and nearby hills are named: Tabor, Zion, Horeb, Golgotha. This is why Wambierzyce is called Silesian Jerusalem.

WARSAW ŁAZIENKI PARK

Warsaw *Łazienki* Park, also called Royal Łazienki Park, was a summer residence of Stanisław August Poniatowski, the last king of Poland, in the
18th century. Once located far from the city today is almost in the centre of Warsaw.

Łazienki Park dates back to construction of castle in
Ujazdów on the other side of *Agrykola* Street. Ujazdów
castle was erected at the beginning of the 17th century as
a royal residence of king Sigismund III Vasa. Later in the
17th century the castle was bought by Grand Marshal of
the Crown Stanisław Herakliusz Lubomirski, who in the
small coppice below the castle built two pavilions – Ere-
mity and Palace (Bath). The bath house was established
on the isle in Baroque style designed by Tylman van Gameren. Inside there was a round room covered with peb-
bles and shells, with a fountain in the centre. It is from
the bath house built by Lubomirski that the surrounding
area took name *Łazienki* (Polish equivalent of *baths*).

In 1764 Ujazdów became the property of the king
Stanisław August Poniatowski, who immediately ordered
refurbishment of the residence and of the nearby park.
A 5 km long entry avenue was set up, later determining
urban layout of this part of Warsaw. New facilities were

erected in the Park, i.e. White House, Old Orangery or Myślewicki Palace. Palace on the Water (bath house) was also altered into a representative small palace. The main designers were court architects of the king: Domenico Merlini and Johann Christian Kamsetzer.

At the times of Stanisław August Poniatowski rules Łazienki was a park opened to Warsaw inhabitants. A theatre (so-called Theatre on the Water) gave performances for about 1000 spectators. During partitions of Poland *Łazienki* became the property of tsars of Russia. The Park, rebuilt after destruction of the II world war, is one of the largest and most beautiful parks of Warsaw.

The history of palace in Wilanów dates back to 1677, when Milanów, a village near Warsaw, became the property of John III Sobieski (*Jan III Sobieski*). According to current fashion its name was changed to Villa Nova. With the passing of time the name was polonized to Wilanów.

The first building constructed by the order of the king was one-storey manor designed by Augustyn Wincenty Locci, court architect of John III Sobieski. Soon after the manor had been modernized and rebuilt to become a residence suitable for the Commonwealth's monarch. As a consequence of works started in 1677 and finished in 1696 a new building appeared with characteristic features of noble manor, Italian villa and French palace in Louis XIV style. Apart from decorative character, external and internal decoration of the residence played the role glorifying the king. Main body of the palace is decorated with bas-reliefs with battle pieces, election and coronation scenes as well as sculptures of ancient gods, symbolizing virtues of the Wilanów owner.

The palace is surrounded by beautiful gardens including also the lake Jezioro Wilanowskie and flowing stream Potok Służewiecki. Gardens were arranged in different styles, e.g. two-level Baroque garden, English scenic garden, neo-Renaissance rose garden and scenic park in English and Chinese style.

After the death of king Sobieski the palace was taken over by Elżbieta Sieniawska, a founder of side wings of the residence. Subsequently the palace was inherited by the families of Lubomirski, Potocki and Branicki, the latter being the last private owner of Wilanów until 1944.

The palace and park in Wilanów is a priceless testimony of the splendour of Polish culture, and one of the most beautiful Baroque residences in Europe. At present it is also a place for cultural events and concerts.

WIELICZKA SALT MINE

Historic salt mine in Wieliczka is the only mine in the world in continuous operation since Medieval times. Mine pits are ca. 300 km long and run on nine levels down to the depth 327 m. The fact that Wieliczka mine is an example of mining engineering development on subsequent historic stages, helped to enter Wieliczka on UNESCO World Heritage List as the site among first twelve world's sites in 1978.

Already since Medieval times salt mine in Wieliczka was an economic foundation for the Polish state. Salt was a very expensive commodity, often used as a means of payment. It is estimated that in the 14th century salt mines brought about one third of all country's revenues, allowing to provide for royal court and to fund construction of castles.

In the 19th century attention has been paid to medical properties of saline baths and the first bathing facility was opened in Wieliczka. At present, a sanatorium operates at the depth of 135 m, mostly treating diseases of respiratory tracts.

The tourist route open to sightseers is only a small fraction of the entire mine. The most famous places in the mine is the largest underground temple in the world –

St. Kinga Chapel – 54 m long, 10 m high and 15 m wide. It was laid out in 1896, in the space created after the excavation of a huge green salt block. It was furnished by miner sculptors, who out of salt blocks made altars, figures of saints and miners and bas-reliefs representing scenes from New Testament. Other interesting places are: the oldest of all preserved underground chapels – St. Anthony Chapel from the 17th century, or the highest (50 m high) Stanisław Staszic Chamber.

WIGRY

Monastic complex of the Congregation of Monk Hermits of Camaldoli on the Wigry lake is one of the most beautiful monuments of Suwałki Region. The area where the buildings are situated was originally an island, separated from the land by a narrow inlet. Such the location protected well against enemies; already in early Mediaeval times the island was inhabited by a tribe of Yotvingians.

In 1667 the Wigry lake and surrounding forest were granted to the congregation of hermits by the king John II Casimir of Poland. Immediately after arriving the monks commenced the construction of the church and residential and farm buildings. In 1671 all buildings constructed until that moment were destroyed by fire. However, the monks quickly restored the monastery. In the years 1694–1745 according to a design of Piotr Puttini the St. Mary Assumption Baroque church was built furnished in very artistic and rich manner.

Bringing the monks helped to develop the economy of this region. Monks were building mills, pitchers and breweries, put beehives in trees. Thanks to efficient administration of the estates in the second half of the 18th century the monks were the owners of the town Suwałki, 11 granges, 56 villages, 6 mills and 404 beehives.

In 1796 Prussian authorities confiscated the congregation property and a few years later expelled monks from Wigry. Until present day legends are told about treasures hidden in huge basements under the monastery. Homeless monks found shelter in Warsaw-Bielany in the fellow monastery.

After abandoning the place monastic buildings deteriorated. First serious reconstruction works were undertaken in the twenties and thirties of the 20th century, but during the II world war the buildings were destroyed again. At present the monastic complex is being restored and makes a tourist attraction in north-eastern Poland.

WROCŁAW

Wroclaw is one of the oldest and largest cities in Poland. Most probably it was founded in early 10th century by Duke Vratislav I of Bohemia (*Wratysław*). It is traditionally believed that the city was named after him. In late 10th century the city passed into the hands of Piast dynasty. In the year 1000 king Boleslaw I of Poland established the first bishopric of Silesia, which the year is considered as the city foundation date.

The town was given Magdeburg rights several times in Middle Ages. During Mongol invasion in 1241 Wroclaw was abandoned and burnt. During rebuilding Market Square was marked out, new streets expanded and new foundation rights granted. In the 14th century Wroclaw broke ties with Poland, and the city declared an economic war with Cracow. In 1741 Wroclaw passed into hands of Prussia and soon was granted a Royal City status after Berlin and Kaliningrad (former Königsberg or Królewiec in Polish). During II World War German army transformed Wroclaw into a fortress which was defended longer than Berlin. Almost 70% of buildings was destroyed during war operations.

Despite war destruction many precious historical buildings survived or was restored. In particular, the Gothic Town Hall and numerous churches, e.g. John the Baptist cathedral, Holy Cross church, Main Railway Station (Dworzec Główny) in Neo-Gothic style or a complex of University buildings including the Leopoldine Hall, a Baroque hall of honour. An interesting building entered on the list of UNESCO World Heritage is the People's Hall (*Hala Ludowa*) also known as Centential Hall (*Hala Stulecia*) designed for popular events by the modernist architect Max Berg, at the beginning of the 20th century. At that time it was an innovative structure with the world largest reinforced concrete roofing. The Hall could seat over 10,000 people.

A curiosity of Wroclaw, a town on Oder river, is the number of bridges and footbridges giving the city a fourth position in Europe after Amsterdam, Venice and Saint Petersburg.

ZALIPIE A PAINTED VILLAGE

Zalipie is a small village in south-eastern Poland, which became an ethnographic curiosity and regional legend. The village was famous at the beginning of the 20th century thanks to general interest in folk culture and Władysław Hickel, whose servant boy was from Zalipie. The boy had got with him a hand-painted small tapestry, a family gift. Delighted with the tapestry Hickel decided to find its place of origin. As a consequence of his search he published his observations in a magazine "Lud" (*People*), and a collection of folk art brought by him aroused general interest.

A habit of painting the farmyards is related to decline of smoke huts and introducing more modern stoves conveying the smoke straight to chimney. Until this moment soot-dark huts now on were painted white with lime to lighten the interior. Probably a habit of painting white gave rise to interior decoration with simple plant forms. This tradition survived, although a necessity to paint the hut white died out. With the passing of time painted ornaments appeared not only inside but also outside and on other farm buildings. Large-size geometrical and floral motives prevailed. Dyes used the most often were: lime, kaolin and soot.

In order to preserve slowly decaying tradition of hut painting a competition for woman painters from the region of the Vistula and Dunajec rivers interfluves took place in 1948. Thanks to charismatic artist Felicja Curyło, Zalipie became a representative village of the region and was called "a painted village". In the seventies of the 20th century a Woman Painters' House (*Dom Malarek*) was established here maintaining the tradition of decorating the farmyard and teaching a new generation of folk woman painters.

ZAMOŚĆ

Zamość was set up in 1580 by Jan Zamojski, a chancellor and great marshal of the crown. A general plan of the town was designed by Italian architect Bernardo Morando. The town was erected according to the plan, adapting it to the needs of the multi-task centre, making Zamość a "perfect" town. It was designed as a family residence, a stronghold, centre of jurisdiction and trade, educational and multi-religious centre. In mid 17th century Zamość fortress fought back Swedish attacks and Cossack forces led by Bohdan Chmielnicki (*Khmelnytsky*). Some time later the town lost its significance. In 1821 Zamoyski family sold the town to the government which enlarged the town and fortified it. Zamość fortress played an important role in the November Uprising in 1830–1831.

Often Zamość is called the "pearl of Renaissance" or "Padua of North", because there are many historic objects originated in that period in this town. Unchanged until these days architectural plan of the Old Town was the main reason to enter the town on the UNESCO World Heritage List. The most important buildings are: a cathedral erected between 1587–1598 and a typical Renaissance Town Hall with late Baroque stairs opening to the main market square. The Market Square of size 100 x 100 m is an urban planning masterpiece. Particularly interesting are arcade houses surrounding the square, designed by Bernard Morand who took Italian Renaissance town houses as a model. Worth visiting are: Zamość Academy (*Akademia Zamojska*), a synagogue, town gates and fortifications.

PHOTO CAPTIONS

S. 4: Temple of Diana, a sculpture in the park.
S. 5: maiolica art workshop, a stone arch.
S. 6: a courtyard with staircase, south-west tower.
S. 7: a mascaron, east façade, a courtyard gallery.
S. 8: border mountain range, a wolf.
S. 9: Orthodox church in Szczawne, Szeroki Wierch (*Wide Peak*).
S. 10: reconstructed settlements, oak-trunk palisade.
S. 11: a fragment of bulwark with tower, entrance gate, a view from lake side.
S. 12: the town hall, the Castle of the Silesian Piast Dynasty.
S. 13: gate of the Castle of the Silesian Piast dynasty.
S. 14: mineral water pump room, a sculpture of "Jaś and Małgosia", salt graduation tower.
S. 15: salt graduation tower.
S. 16: basilica's vault, the miraculous icon of the Virgin Mary (*Black Madonna of Częstochowa*), organ.
S. 17: entrance gate and Jasna Góra tower.
S. 18: a view from Zalew Leśniański side, the castle room.
S. 19: moat and castle façade, south wall, lower courtyard gate.
S. 20: cathedral hill, Frombork panorama with a view of the Vistula Lagoon.
S. 21: fronton of the cathedral, Radziejowski's Tower, cathedral pulpit, cathedral vault.
S. 22: a view from the side of Motława river, Abbots Palace (*Pałac Opacki*) in Oliwa.
S. 23: harbour crane, the Monument of the Fallen Shipyard Workers (*Pomnik Poległych Stoczniowców*), Great Armoury House (*Wielka Zbrojownia*).
S. 24: Długa Street and Golden Gate, Gdańsk coat of arms – house decoration.
S. 25: Neptune fountain, stone decoration in Długi Targ Street, Uphagen's House, Court of Artus.
S. 26: castle view from northern side, west façade.
S. 27: tower and south wing of the castle.
S. 28: viewing deck on Szczeliniec Wielki, "Monkey" – an interesting rock shape, Szczeliniec Wielki top.
S. 29: solitary tree over precipice.
S. 30: monastery on Łysa Góra, the chapel of Oleśnicki family.
S. 31: Góry Świętokrzyskie mountain range, boulder field on Łysa Góra slope.
S. 32: richly decorated interior of the Church of Peace, the castle of Piasts.
S. 33: a tower of the Church of Peace.
S. 34 houses near Town Hall Square (*Plac Ratuszowy*), a fountain with Neptune statue.
S. 35: town hall, penitential cross at the outskirts of town, the interior of the Holy Cross church.
S. 36: sanctuary of the Virgin Mary, station of the Way of the Cross.
S. 37: the Great Passion Play taking place in Holy Week.
S. 38: a boat on slipway cradle, slipway mechanism, a boat in canal.
S. 39: pulling the boat up on slipway.
S. 40: base transceiver station in Śnieżny Kocioł, the Wang temple.
S. 41: a tourist shelter on Śnieżka mountain top, Szklarka Waterfall, Karkonosze Mountains.
S. 42: castle ruins, a house in Kazimierz.
S. 43: a house in the Market Square, a granary of Ulanowski family, Jews Memorial on former Jewish Cemetery, parish church.
S. 44: Kłodzko fortress, St.Mary of the Assumption Parish Church.
S. 45: a town view from Kłodzko fortress, town hall, Gothic St. John's bridge.
S. 46: Mauritanian room, ceiling in a Coat of Arm's room.
S. 47: garden-side façade of the castle.
S. 48: the Cloth Hall in Market Square, Juliusz Słowacki Theatre.
S. 49: a hansom cab in front of St.Mary's Church, the Cloth Hall view from the south, St. Adalbert's Church.
S. 50: Wawel view from the side of Dębnicki Bridge, Byzantine paintings on a vault of Świętokrzyska Chapel.
S. 51: Gothic defence tower, Wawel Cathedral, Renaissance castle courtyard.
S. 52: castle view from the side of gardens, courtyard.
S. 53: royal donjon, screen wall, courtyard decorations.
S. 54: Cistercian abbey view, stations of the Way of the Cross.
S. 55: penitential cross, station of the Way of the Cross, painted ceiling of the abbey church.
S. 56: southern side of the castle, a balcony in the Maximilian Room.
S. 57: a fireplace in the Maximilian Room, stone decorations in south-west castle wing, castle gardens.
S. 58: "Herring" houses, the Castle of Piasts.
S. 59: a church in Legnickie Pole, a house "Pod Przepiórczym Koszem".
S. 60: Basilica of Our Lady of Licheń, entrance stairs to the Basilica.
S. 61: statue of St. Michael Archangel, Basilica interior.
S. 62: the castle of Warmian bishops, Gothic room in the castle.
S. 63: St.Peter&Paul Orthodox Church, donjon in the Warmian Bishops Castle, castle galleries.
S. 64: Grodzka Gate view, Cracow Gate, Podwale Street.
S. 65: Jewish Cemetery, Old Town view from the east, Castle Square.
S. 66: the castle from the West Bridge side, a cupola.
S. 67: the castle from Italian Garden side, a tower, a sculpture from the Italian Garden.
S. 68: panorama of the castle from west side, Palace of the Great Masters of the Order and castle church.
S. 69: ivy-overgrown castle window, a room in the Palace of the Great Masters, stone decoration, galleries.
S. 70: lake pier, at dawn.
S. 71: lakeshore, Masurian navigable route.
S. 72: panorama of the castle from park side, south façade.
S. 73: stone decoration, the palace from the south-east side, the staircase.

S. 74: castle panorama from the side of Czorsztyn Reservoir, a balcony in the courtyard.
S. 75: southern donjon.
S. 76: castle panorama from town side, castle view from north-west side.
S. 77: a donjon, stone decoration, castle chapel vault.
S. 78: panorama of Pieniny Mountains from the west, Sokolica top.
S. 79: Dunajec River rafting, solitary tree on Sokolica top, a view of Dunajec River and Trzy Korony peaks.
S. 80: the castle and Gate Tower, the Club of Hercules (*Maczuga Herkulesa*), a clock on castle façade.
S. 81: Italian Gardens on terrace.
S. 82: town hall, cathedral Basilica.
S. 83: Mariavite Temple of Mercy and Charity (*Świątynia Miłosierdzia i Miłości*), Clock Tower, castle hill with a view of Vistula River.
S. 84: tenement houses on the Market Square, town hall decorations.
S. 85: Renaissance town hall, Bamberki well, Franciscan church.
S. 86: aerial view of the Peninsula, a lighthouse in Hel.
S. 87: fisherman's cabin, harbour in Hel.
S. 88: town panorama from the castle side, castle gate.
S. 89: a statue in front of Franciscan church, archiepiscopal chapel, decorations of houses in the Market Square, tower of archiepiscopal church.
S. 90: bell tower, window and wooden roofing tiles, wall paintings inside the temple.
S. 91: Orthodox church from south-west side.
S. 92: palace from the east, a garden sculpture.
S. 93: Rogalin oak tres.
S. 94: castle view from the Old Town, city promenade and the Holy Cross Church.
S. 95: towers of the town hall, defence walls of Rzeszów castle, summer palace of the Lubomirski family.
S. 96: west façade of the castle, Renaissance town hall.
S. 97: Renaissance house, interior of the cathedral, town panorama from right bank of the Vistula River.
S. 98: a dune, Łabsko Lake, a lighthouse in Czołpino.
S. 99: migrating dunes.
S. 100: town view from the pier, balneological facility.
S. 101: Grand Hotel, a house in town's centre, a pier in Sopot.
S. 102: aqueducts, bridge span.
S. 103: aqueduct view from the valley's bottom.
S. 104: Suwałki landscape, erratic field.
S. 105: forest road, erratic field, Hańcza Lake.
S. 106: Wały Chrobrego view from Castle Route overpass, Pomeranian Dukes' Castle.
S. 107: houses in Podzamcze Street, Wały Chrobrego, a fountain on Wały Chrobrego.
S. 108: castle ruins in Ogrodzieniec, remains of castle tower in Olsztyn, castle ruins in Ogrodzieniec.
S. 109: castle ruins in Mirów.
S. 110: houses in Market Square, the Church of Peace.
S. 111: sculptures decorating the Cathedral, St.Stanislaus & Adalbert Cathedral, Baroque interior of the Church of Peace.
S. 112: Basilica in Święta Lipka, painting on gallery vaults.
S. 113: galleries, organ.
S. 114: Renaissance town hall, decoration of city houses.
S. 115: houses in Market Square.
S. 116: a mosque in Bohoniki, *mizar* (cemetery) in Bohoniki.
S. 117: a mosque in Kruszyniany.
S. 118: mountain range, a view of Giewont.
S. 119: Tatra Mountains from Gubałówka, Morskie Oko Lake in winter, a view of east part of Tatra Mountains, Roztoka Stream.
S. 120: Siklawa Waterfall, mountain cabin, Roztoka Valley.
S. 121: Great Polish Lake (*Wielki Staw Polski*).
S. 122: bridge view from the river, tower and spans.
S. 123: decorated bridge tower.
S. 124: Teutonic castle, town view from the town hall tower.
S. 125: town hall, monument of Nicolas Copernicus, the Court of Artus.
S. 126: Holy Trinity Church from the other side of the Narew River, Great Synagogue.
S. 127: the synagogue's interior.
S. 128: St. Mary Visitation Church, station of the Way of the Cross.
S. 129: paintings on the Basilica vault, a view of the Basilica and Stołowe Mountains, stations of the Way of the Cross.
S. 130: Łazienki Palace, monument of Frederic Chopin.
S. 131: a sculpture in front of Łazienki Palace, a faun in the park, the Orangery (*Stara Pomarańczarnia*).
S. 132: palace fronton, mausoleum of Potocki family.
S. 133: a sundial, a sculpture in the park, decorations of the palace annexe.
S. 134: Kunegunda's shaft station, miner's symbol.
S. 135: Christ's statue, Daniłowicz shaft, salt-sculpted Last Supper in St. Kinga Chapel.
S. 136: panorama of Camaldolese Monastery from Wigry Lake, alley running between monk hermitages.
S. 137: hermitages of monks, monastery tower.
S. 138: hansom cab in front of the town hall, towers of the St. John the Baptist Cathedral located on Ostrów Tumski Isle, Baroque Hall Aula Leopoldina.
S. 139: a house "Pod Siedmioma Elektorami", town hall window, town hall sculptures.
S. 140: a painted hut, a colourful beehive.
S. 141: a well sweep, an ornament, painted hut windows.
S. 142: the house "Pod Aniołem", ramparts of Zamość fortress.
S. 143: Renaissance town hall.